Success — What Does It Take?

Kendall M. Handy, M.D.

Copyright © 2012 by Kendall M. Handy, M.D.

Success-What Does It Take?
by Kendall M. Handy, M.D.

Printed in the United States of America

ISBN 9781625090102

All rights reserved solely by the author. The author guarantees all contents are original and do not infringe upon the legal rights of any other person or work. No part of this book may be reproduced in any form without the permission of the author. The views expressed in this book are not necessarily those of the publisher.

Unless otherwise indicated, Bible quotations are taken from the New International Version of the Bible. Copyright 1996 by Zondervan Publishing House.

Credit for front cover picture of Kendall Handy to Kimhummel.com

www.xulonpress.com

For Janet, Kendra, Carldarone, Lauren, Rorey, and Gloria

ACKNOWLEDGMENTS

Wow, where do I start? I have to thank my parents for going to work every day and helping me to experience music, sports, and education. We didn't have any long conversations regarding life and how to live it, but their example of getting up every day and going to work laid the foundation for me to realize that a big part of success is working to get what you want. I am also fortunate to have been born into an extended family of teachers, and hard-working aunts, uncles, cousins, and sisters. Is this a big deal? Of course it is. It means I have been conditioned by a fertile environment that says get your butt out of bed and go do something to make money so that you can eat. So I have been extremely blessed with a strong village.

I have been attending Christian Churches all my life. That's over 50 years of listening to how you should treat others, how to work, play, love, forgive, and give grace to everyone. I was far from perfect, but thank God I knew where the track was when I got off track. The first self-help book I ever read would have to be the Bible. Thank God for giving me the desire to read it and learn from it. I thank all the ministers and pastors that have spoken a word from the pulpit as I sat there taking notes or falling asleep (I was awake most of the time).

I have read or listened to over a hundred self-help books, and the first secular self-help book I ever read was "Your Erroneous Zones" by Dr. Wayne Dyer back when I was in either high school or college. After reading it I kept reading and growing and looking for ways to simply develop me. I read so many books and gained so much information that now I look forward to sharing all that I've learned with whoever will listen.

My wife Janet has been my biggest cheerleader, and I thank God for her support as she watched me start and stop and start this project over and over without questioning why it was taking me so long and why was I procrastinating on a book that talks about getting things done. I love you Janet and thank you for your encouragement. It's time for you to write your book. I'll help.

Finally, I have to admit that I simply love people and the things they do that inspire me to be better every day at whatever I might be doing. People can be crazy, annoying, and just bad sometimes, but there are plenty of great people who we can all learn from and gain the inspiration that can take us to new heights. So thanks to all the people who get up every day and live this life that is full of challenges. I thank God for life and this great country where you can read a book, and with the knowledge gained achieve just about anything.

CONTENTS

Dedication v
Acknowledgements vii
Introduction xi
Chapter One: Discipline 13
Chapter Two: Take Action 25
Chapter Three: Make the Mistakes 36
Chapter Four: Practice 44
Chapter Five: Courage 51
Chapter Six: Plan to Succeed 63
Chapter Seven: It's Hard 69
Chapter Eight: Develop Good Habits 79
Chapter Nine: Slow Down 88
Chapter Ten: It's On You 96
Conclusion 105

Introduction

I have been reading self-help books for over thirty years. During most of that time I was looking for the secret to success. Of course, there are no secrets but only simple fundamental concepts, habits, and behaviors that successful people develop, exhibit, and utilize on a daily basis. One needs to be aware of certain actions and behaviors that lead to success, and once you apply these similar principles, you too can be on your way to greater success. I must warn you up front that being successful is not easy for anyone. If it were easy you probably wouldn't be interested in it, and everybody would be trying to be successful.

I think a lot of people who are looking to be successful know that it isn't easy but they just need to keep hearing that from multiple reliable sources. That's why I like to read biographies about high achievers. When you read about great athletes, presidents, musicians, artists, CEOs and the like, remember that they are humans just like you. They struggle and have similar fears. High achievers have to have courage to do and achieve what they do. They have to take action and persevere every day. It wasn't easy, and it took time for them to reach their goals. We see their success but often don't sit and ponder about how much it takes for them to be successful.

Let's get right to one point. You will need courage to read this book. You may have read several self-help books in the past, and you may be afraid that this will be one more book that you read and no change occurs. You may be afraid that you still won't find out what it takes to be successful. I can assure you that this book has the fundamentals you'll need to be a major success at whatever you do. You need courage to read this book because you may be afraid that this is going to be one more self-help book that wants you to think positive and follow your passion. Positive thinking and passion are two ingredients to success, but it takes much more than that. Just like sugar and flour are major ingredients for making a cake, it takes more than that if you want an edible cake. I can assure you this book will tell you what it takes to get the job done. Yes, it will be preachy. I admit that I will need to be in your face with some of this information, and that's what I believe most people looking to improve themselves want. You want to know what will give you real results. You may only learn one new concept from this book, and that's alright. That one piece of information could be the one thing you needed to hear to catapult you to the next level.

I am of the opinion that people need to work at something to have a fulfilling life. That doesn't mean they need to write the next great novel or climb the highest peak, but it means that people who have a desire to accomplish something get a tremendous amount of satisfaction in life if they do reach certain goals they have for themselves. You may want to be a better teacher, lawyer, auto mechanic, athlete, parent, or spouse yet you're wondering what it would take for you to be much better. My goal is to give you that one more ingredient you may be missing or all the ingredients you'll need to help you reach your goals.

I need and want you to remember there are no shortcuts to success. No whining, no quitting, no easy roads to real success. You will have to apply everything you read about in this book not only once but all the time if you want to be successful. Not only that, but you have to continue to apply the following disciplines consistently in order to maintain your level of success. That's why you will want to make the characteristic and traits of the successful person a habit. I will cover developing habits in this book and talk about the importance of them to your success.

Success doesn't happen overnight. You will need to take small steps every single day in the direction of your goals if you want to be successful. It's been said that the things we need to do are easy to do. The problem is that they are also easy not to do. Again, if it were too easy everyone would be successful. So in the interest of your time and so that you can begin your journey toward success, let's get going.

Chapter One

Discipline

Accomplishing anything worthwhile requires discipline. You have to be able to make yourself complete the task at hand, within the timeline you've promised yourself. Often, we don't do that which we know we should do, because we don't *feel* like doing it. We may be afraid of failure—or success—or we simply don't feel like moving. We may be too tired or lack the motivation to act on a particular day, yet we still have a goal to reach. When this happens, we need to discipline ourselves to act regardless of how we feel. Being disciplined means making yourself do something even though you don't feel like doing it.

When a writer sits down to write for three or four hours Monday through Friday, she doesn't always feel like writing. A writer disciplines herself to sit down and write because otherwise her book would never get finished. If she waited for that special feeling to come along, she would never get anything written. When I started writing, I consistently wanted the stars to line up and the gates of heaven to pour perfect sentences into my head to be transcribed on paper. Guess what? It didn't happen, because life doesn't work that way. I had to learn to sit my butt in a chair and write. I always felt great after I finished, but it was often stressful to sit and write regardless of my feelings. It also didn't feel good to sit and stare at a blank page, but that is a part of the process.

There is no magic pill. You must get yourself to do that which you desire to do, and that which you are required to do. John Maxwell states in his book, *Developing the Leader Within*, that "all great leaders have understood that their number one responsibility was for their own discipline and personal growth." We have to develop this trait in our lives as soon as possible. This is a trait that moves us from desire to results. You have to be the one who makes yourself get out of bed, read the spreadsheet, exercise, or change your eating habits. It's great to have friends and family who encourage us to achieve our goals, but they aren't going to be there at 5:00 AM telling you to get up and start working or exercising. That's going to be up to you.

There's something called emotional discipline; this discipline is what Charles Manz describes as "the power to choose how you feel." The importance of emotional discipline is its ability to motivate one to action, knowing that those actions will lead you toward the positive feelings you want to have. When I think about writing, I don't always feel like sitting down and writing. I sometimes catch myself emptying out the dishwasher, rather than sitting down and writing. Sometimes, I have to get myself to think about how good it's going to feel once I finish writing several pages. I usually feel better once I actually sit down and start writing. The problem is getting me to sit down and write. I want to *feel* like writing, studying, practicing, or reading, but one can't always rely on feelings to be present before taking action. As a matter of fact, you can rarely rely on the right feelings to be present.

You're more likely to act yourself into feeling than feel yourself into action.

—Jerome Bruner

The above quote is one of the most powerful statements I've ever read, because you will rarely feel your way into doing anything. You must act, and know that your feelings will come and go, but at least you'll be achieving what you want to achieve. You'll start feeling better about yourself when you take action doing what you don't feel like doing. This is having discipline. Kelly Stone wrote a book called *Time to Write* in which she talks about a time when she had planned to do some writing in a nice quiet place at home but roofers came to work on her house that day. They were making a lot of noise, and she was tempted not to do any writing. In her words she says "I reminded myself that successful writers write no matter what." I think this can be carried over to other disciplines. Successful musicians and athletes often practice no matter what. People often procrastinate because they're waiting to feel like doing

Discipline

a task rather than simply doing it. Think of all those times you felt down or depressed because it happened to be raining, yet once you started doing something or taking action you felt better. It didn't have to stop raining for you to feel better, it took action.

As long as you can start, you are alright. The juice will come.
— Ernest Hemingway

I make myself sit and write, knowing that I'll feel good about what I've accomplished after I get finished. But sometimes that isn't enough. Discipline requires that you take action whether you are psyched up to or not. Discipline doesn't care about feelings, the muse, your headache, or anything else. Discipline just wants action toward your goals. Think about the confidence you'll have if you know that when you tell yourself that you are going to do something, you do it and there is no doubt about whether it is going to get done or not. Let's say you plan to get up and exercise tomorrow at 5:00 AM. You know that it will get done, and it will not matter how you feel or how tired you are because when you say you'll do something you do it no matter what.

It's important to focus on how you want to feel versus how you currently feel because you'll rarely feel like doing certain task that require either thinking or physical exertion. Writing, reading, exercising, and studying are some of the activities we want to do, but don't initially feel like doing. We love to be finished doing the above activities, and we get a great deal of satisfaction from completing them; however, we procrastinate because we don't feel like performing the above task.

We procrastinate because of a lack of discipline. Putting things off usually occurs because we're currently not in the mood to start the task. The question is when will you be in the mood? Procrastinating doesn't bring on the mood or provide any motivation for getting the job done. Acting in spite of your current mood is what gets things done. This requires self-discipline.

Stephen King is the author of more than thirty books. Several of them have been made into movies. In his book *On Writing,* he talks of his routine of writing everyday when he's working on a novel. That would even include Christmas, the Fourth of July, and his birthday. He says in his book "I like to get ten pages a day, which amounts to 2,000 words." ". . . only under dire circumstances do I allow myself to shut down before I get my 2,000 words."

Now that takes discipline.

In medical school, I couldn't afford to wait until the last minute to prepare for an exam. I made sure that I started studying early to be thoroughly prepared for my test. Did I feel like studying? Sometimes yes, but oftentimes not. I couldn't afford not to study simply because I didn't feel like it. I was mindful of the consequences of not studying and how bad it would feel to get a bad grade because I lacked the discipline to study.

In the last analysis, our only freedom is the freedom to discipline ourselves.

—Bernard Baruch

Discipline is not a bad word. It is not the enemy. Discipline is the key ingredient that has to be added to any plan for success. Without discipline you won't make a plan, and if you do have a plan, you won't follow it through to completion. You can have a strong desire and that desire can carry you a long way, but there are times when the emotions stirred by desire are not enough. You will have to make yourself get out of bed, exercise, write, study, read, or do whatever you have planned to do.

To achieve anything in this world requires action. Discipline and action are bedfellows. A lack of action usually means the lack of discipline to take action. As George Bernard Shaw has said, "self-control is the quality that distinguishes the fittest to survive." Just think about how much you could accomplish if you actually did what you wanted to do versus what you felt like doing. Wouldn't it be wonderful if you had that kind of confidence in yourself? Wouldn't it be great to consistently follow through on your plans?

All of us are afraid of something at some time or another in our lives. Fear is a part of being alive. Courage happens when we discipline ourselves to act in spite of our fears. Discipline requires courage. I was afraid of failure when I applied to medical school—afraid that I would not get in. After I got into school I was afraid I wouldn't have what it takes to stay in medical school. But in spite

Discipline

of these fears I took action and made myself do what I had to do. Courage requires discipline. You have to discipline yourself to act in spite of the fear. Perseverance requires discipline. Acquiring knowledge requires discipline. Anything worth having is going to require discipline to achieve. Look at some of the problems we can have because of our lack of discipline.

1. Debt—we buy what we cannot afford.
2. Obesity—we eat too much.
3. Poor health—not exercising, eating poorly.
4. Depressed mood—feeling down because of inaction.
5. Sin—disobedience regarding the Ten Commandments.
6. Failure—not doing what needed to be done.

When I go to the doctors' lounge for lunch the first item to choose from is dessert. I love dessert. Cakes, pies, puddings, you name it and I like it. But, I can't afford to eat dessert every day at lunch. Maybe back in my teenage years I could get away with it, but not now. I have to use major self-control to keep from eating the forbidden fruit. This is where the discipline of not doing something comes into play. I have to tell myself to step away from the bread pudding. It's not always easy and sometimes it' just hard to do, but discipline requires us to make the hard choices. Not using that credit card, not overeating, not being selfish, not drinking too much or, well, you fill in the blank. All of the above require discipline.

Self-discipline is a quality that is won through practice.
—John C. Maxwell

We can develop a habit of being disciplined. Start by making yourself do small task on a regular basis. You may need to carve out a particular time to read, write, walk, clean house, or any number of tasks. Tell yourself that you are going to do the particular task for at least thirty minutes. *How you feel does not matter*. I find that I often don't feel like doing most of the chores that I want to get done. Discipline yourself to do what you want to do but don't feel like doing. What matters is getting the task done. There are going to be times when you are going to be tired. I'm tired all the time.

I'm tired at three o'clock in the morning when the nurse calls me to do a delivery. That mother about to deliver doesn't want to hear about how tired I am. She wants that baby out, and it's my job to get out of bed and help her get it out. Being tired is one of the biggest excuses for not doing what needs to be done. That's why it's so important to get enough exercise and sleep in order to reduce the chances of using fatigue as an excuse. You can't allow feelings and fatigue to get in the way of your thirty minutes of getting the task done. Sometimes we are tired because what we know we should be doing is wearing us down. If thirty minutes seems too long then give yourself ten minutes to do part of a task and you'll be surprised at how much you get done and how much better you'll feel.

I often get up at 5:00 AM on weekdays to put in at least thirty minutes of exercise. I don't feel like doing it most mornings. I do it because exercise is good for my body and helps me deal with the stresses of daily life. If I got up when I felt like it I would never get any exercise done. Now, I'm not saying that feelings are bad. Feelings and emotions add flavor to our lives, but we have to discern when our feelings are working for us or against us. We don't feel good when we procrastinate and miss an opportunity to advance in some area of interest all because we didn't *feel* like taking action. Successful people take action. They are disciplined and do what needs to be done right now. Successful people don't wait for some warm and fuzzy time in the future. They know it's not coming any time soon. I can't afford to wait for the muse; neither can any artist afford to wait until the muse arrives. The muse arrives because the artist sits down and begins. This requires discipline.

"Successful people do what unsuccessful people are not willing to do."

-Darren Hardy

Are you waiting to get motivated before you begin that exercise regiment or learn a foreign language or start that diet; well, guess what—you need to *just do it*. The motivation you're looking for will come, but only after you make it come by taking action. Taking action in the direction of your goals is the best way to get motivated. Let motivation come while you're running, dieting, writing, or doing

Discipline

whatever you need to be doing to reach your goals. We can control our emotional destiny by acting now, and not being a slave to some emotion that may or may not come. I remember studying four to five hours at a time when I was in college. During these times I would have feelings of satisfaction come over me such that I loved having large blocks of time to study. It was like a runner's high—that great feeling that runners get when they've logged in several miles and they feel good about being out and doing what they set out to do. They feel like they could keep running forever.

Let discipline become a habit for you. Without it we waste a lot of time wishing we would do this or that. Again, just do it. Kick procrastination to the curb. Once you start moving in the direction of success, you'll start to feel good about yourself and what you're doing. And please, please, please don't let this go in one ear and out the other. Take action and see for yourself how good you feel when you do what you've been called to do and want to do. You will not benefit from all the self-help books in the world if you don't make yourself do what those books tell you to do. A preacher can preach until he's blue in the face about our need to pray, fellowship, or read God's word, but if we can't get ourselves to do it, we will never grow spiritually. We have to be bold enough to live a disciplined life. A life full of rewards and accomplishments is born out of making yourself do what needs to be done.

A habit doesn't require you to constantly make yourself do something, but it moves you toward doing things automatically. It takes willpower to initiate the habit of exercising, but once you develop the habit you need less willpower and begin to exercise because it has become a part of your routine. They say it takes about twenty-one days to establish a new habit. Sometimes it takes longer, but on average if you can make yourself get into the routine of disciplining yourself every day, then you will develop positive habits that will help you reach your goals automatically. I must warn you, however, that there are some tasks that you may never feel like doing such as exercising, or getting up early to read, or planning your day. You do these things because success demands they be done and successful people do what success demands to be done. I get up at 5:00 AM to get my workout done, and there are some who get up earlier than that. I rarely feel like getting up that early, but it's the best way for

Success-What Does It Take?

me to take control of my day and get done what I need to get done before my world wakes up. I started getting up earlier because I have read and heard from multiple sources that successful people get up early and take control of their day.

I mentioned willpower earlier. It's not enough to just have willpower. You have to have a strong why for doing what you need to do. Why do you want to lose weight, and why do you want to start a business or write a book? If your why is strong, then your will to achieve will be strong. If your reason for doing something isn't strong enough, you will be at risk of quitting when the going gets tough.

I needed money to help pay tuition for college. I helped perform research on rats and had to lift them up by the tail and place a Q-tip in an area where "the sun don't shine." I had to get up early and do this before class every day for a period of time and hated it. However my why was to get research experience and money for school. My why for doing it gave me the willpower I needed to keep doing what I needed to do, and you will need to define your why for taking action to achieve success.

If you have discipline, you have self-control. When I was in college, I also worked at a grocery store in the evening and would not get home until eleven o'clock at night. I would come home and then study subjects like organic chemistry, and biology until two o'clock in the morning. This became a routine that required me to make myself stay up and study until I knew the material well. I knew that I would be up until at least 2:00 AM studying, and I had confidence that I would get my work done. A little music and a lot of studying has been a disciplined routine that I have had to have from college on through medical school. Coffee didn't help me stay up, although sipping on a cup of it or on a cup of tea gave me something to do while I was studying. What works for me is having self-control. When you have self-control, you will develop self confidence.

The confidence you build within yourself will allow you to tackle whatever problems or projects that come at you.

I truly believe we can become disciplined and enjoy it—after years of practicing it.

—John C. Maxwell

Discipline

Do you have confidence that you will do what you say you're going to do? This confidence only comes from practicing discipline every day. It doesn't come by being disciplined sporadically. I try to write everyday so that it becomes a part of my routine. When I do it every day, it becomes less of a battle to do. I still have to decide that I am going to write that day, however.

You need to practice discipline every day. Practice it until you see the fruit of your labors and then practice it some more. There will be no time in your life when you will not have to practice discipline. Every day you will need to make a conscious decision to do what needs to be done and not just what you feel like doing. I wish I could tell you differently but I can't, and the reason I can't is because in studying about the subject I found that we actually feel better about ourselves when we use discipline. You will enjoy life more and be more fulfilled if you are disciplined versus falling through life being tossed about by your feelings. Think of something you don't feel like doing and then do it. See what it feels like and then recognize that it didn't kill you to do it. For some reason our brains make it seem like we are going to die if we do something we don't feel like doing. You often have to ignore your brain especially when it is preventing you from taking action.

A disciplined life is a life of freedom. Some people think discipline is restrictive because they're making themselves do something they don't feel like doing. But think about all the important things that you could make yourself do that would lead to more freedom such as getting that project done first thing in the morning rather than having to dwell on what you need to be doing all day long. Making yourself organize your work such that it gets done and you will have time to play tennis or go biking or go to the gym. Most of us have the time to do a lot of what we want to do but we simply don't take the time to plan out our days. We often spend a lot of time spinning our wheels rather that making ourselves take action. You wonder why you're bored, and it's because of inaction.

I have colleagues that play golf almost every weekend. They work hard during the week and play hard on the weekend. When I'm at work I work. When you are at work you should try to get as much work done as possible so that your time off can be used for family, friends, and play. If you will discipline yourselves to do this, then everyday you will have a light at the end of the tunnel. You have something to look forward to.

Give yourself something to look forward to after you have worked hard all day. Put some play back into your life. If you are an adult reading this book I want you to think about what you used to do for fun as a child and make yourself get out and be that child again. If you liked riding your bike as a child, then go get a bike and ride it as an adult. If you collected baseball cards, then start collecting again. Make yourself live this life to the fullest. I know that sounds strange but we live in a time where people have become so consumed with working that they have neglected to play and enjoy life. Work is fulfilling but we all need balance and to achieve balance requires making an assessment of where you are and what you are doing, then prioritizing your activities to include work, play, and relaxation.

It takes discipline for me to be relaxed, or to even make the decision to take it easy. I have a tendency to walk, talk, write, and read fast. This creates a lot of unnecessary tension in me that could be avoided by slowing down, however for me to slow down requires conscious effort, which means I have to discipline myself to write my prescriptions slowly, and interview my patients slowly. This is a constant battle. I have to make myself slow down. I'll talk more about slowing down in a later chapter, but right now I want to emphasis the discipline it takes to be in a more relaxed state.

Meditation requires discipline. Have you ever noticed how hard it can be to sit and focus on your breath only? It's a wonderful practice and it requires considerable discipline. Meditation is a great practice to learn because it improves your focus and your discipline in other areas. Think about how your mind likes to wonder off into other areas while you're trying to read this book. Sometimes I'll be reading and after an entire paragraph my mind is somewhere else and I can't recall a thing I just read. I have to go back and reread the paragraph. It's a constant battle we all have. Some people have greater concentration than others and you can develop a higher level of concentration through meditation, but it will require making yourself do the work needed to improve your concentration.

Keeping me together requires a ton of discipline. Working on you requires a ton of discipline. There is a tendency to not want to

Discipline

do anything, and sometimes we do need to not do anything. There should be down time incorporated into every day, but at some point you have to get your work done.

Here are some ways to develop discipline:

1. If you eat three times a day, then take the time to evaluate yourself every time you eat. You could carry an index card on you with the word discipline on it. Morning, noon, and night you look at that card to remind yourself to be disciplined.
2. Give yourself time to develop discipline as a habit. It takes time. It will take longer than the standard twenty-one days to develop this habit. I suggest giving yourself one to two months. This will be an ongoing challenge, but the rewards will be tremendous.
3. Write down the disciplines you want to develop. Make them concrete and refer to the list of disciplines regularly.
4. Read about people who exhibit the traits that you want to have. Find disciplined people you can pattern your life after.
5. Make yourself do something you hate doing every day. It might be exercising, reading a spread sheet, eating a salad, you name it. Just do it. As Brian Tracy says, "eat that frog." The frog is that dreaded action you procrastinate about doing but you know needs to be done.

Your success will depend on your ability to do those tasks that you simply don't like to do. It's easy to do what we want to do, but what separates the great achievers past and present from the average person is this ability to do what they don't feel like doing.

Bottom line: Discipline requires the use of willpower. It takes hard work. Anyone who tells you that being a success is easy, hasn't tried to succeed at anything recently. The sooner you accept the fact that your success is tied to being willing to discipline yourself to do the hard work needed to execute a plan, the sooner you'll reach your goals. I didn't have much time to whine about how much studying I needed to do in medical school. I had to make myself stay up late or get up early to study. There are those who think people who are successful have a special gift that allows them to prosper but that's not the common denominator. The common denominator is hard work. Successful people diligently take action in the direction of their goals.

Talent is overrated is an excellent book written by Geoff Colvin that talks about how it takes *deliberate practice*—and a lot of it—for us to get better at a skill. It takes more than being talented. While others are busy watching, hoping, wishing, and dreaming, successful people are creating plans and executing them. Discipline requires the expenditure of energy. There is no getting around this. This should become a daily way of life. You never reach a point where you don't have to make yourself do what you don't feel like doing. *There are some tasks you will never feel like doing, but you do them anyway because that's what successful people do.* You must embrace discipline the way you hold tightly to courage if you want to reach your goals. Have the courage to make yourself take disciplined action in the fulfillment of your goals. There is no other choice.

Chapter Two

Take Action

The beginning is half of every action.

—Greek proverb

If you want to be successful at anything you must learn to take action. There really isn't any other way. If you're serious about reaching any goal of any kind you need to develop the habit of taking action. The problem most of us have with taking action is not *feeling* like taking action. Think of all the times you wanted to do something but you didn't *feel* like doing it. You want the car cleaned but you don't feel like cleaning it right now. You want to start your own business, but you don't feel like writing out a business plan. You want to lose weight, but you don't feel like exercising or watching your diet.

If you think about it, how often do you actually feel like doing anything? Many of us finished high school, but how many of those twelve years did we feel like being in school? When I think back on it, I know I went to school because my parents expected me to go. It wasn't about what I felt like doing but more about what needed to be done. Some of us would have dropped out of school if we didn't have a parent figure constantly coaching us along. Let's face it, most of us didn't always feel like going to school, yet we did it anyway and accomplished a major milestone in our lives. Finishing high school is a big deal. I like to use that milestone as an example of how many of you can accomplish your goals whether you feel like it or not. You've already shown that you can accomplish something without feeling like it the whole time. You learned to just stick it out.

It takes twelve years to get a high school diploma. If you've done that, give yourself a pat on the back.

We have to be very careful when we allow our feelings to dictate our lives versus allowing what needs to be done to dictate our lives. Our feelings come and go. They are unpredictable. They vary like the wind. Think about it, haven't you ever felt really good when you woke up, but then you turned on the news and heard a bad report? Then all of a sudden you're feeling sad or down about what you just heard. Maybe you were expecting a sunny day, and you woke up to rain instead. Now you start to feel down because it's raining outside. Your entire mood changed. Remember what it felt like to find out that you didn't have school because of the weather? That's probably one of the best feelings in the world. However, something can happen to change that feeling if you let it. If you're feeling down about paying your bills because of a shortage of money, then an unexpected amount of money comes to cover the bill, suddenly you start to feel great.

You have to be careful not to fall victim to feelings that are created by external events—events we often have no control over. We can't afford to allow these events to produce feelings that we then allow to prevent us from reaching our goals.

Never despair, but if you do, work on in despair.
—Edmond Burke

Try to remember that you can create positive feelings by taking actions that you know will bring about the feelings you want to have. For example, let's say you have to study for a major exam or test. You know from prior experience that after you finish studying you feel pretty good. You feel as if you've accomplished something and that you'll be ready for the test. Before you started studying, more often than not, you didn't feel like studying. You probably sat there feeling bad or depressed or guilty because you weren't studying. Now, if you can get yourself to act in spite of your current feelings (we called this emotional discipline earlier), eventually your feelings will change. You may start to have more positive feelings since you'll be doing what you know you should be doing. This change in emotion and feeling occurs because you are accomplishing, or are in the process of achieving, your desired goal. Don't just take my word

Take Action

for this, you need to try it. Do what you don't feel like doing and see how your feelings change after you have been doing it for a while.

People who are high achievers experience positive emotions all the time because they have reversed the feelings—to—action cycle to where their constant actions lead to the positive feelings they want to have. They have developed what Charles C. Manz calls "emotional discipline." Manz wrote a book entitled *Emotional Discipline* in which he describes this discipline as the power to choose how you feel. We can discipline ourselves to take those actions that create positive emotions in us.

When I was in college, there were times when I wished I didn't have to go to sleep. I had so much work to do with going to lectures, studying, and work that I felt I didn't have enough time in my day. I felt sleep was a waste of good study time (this was erroneous thinking because we do need sleep). Once I sat down to study, however, I enjoyed the process. There were many nights when I only got four hours of sleep, but I felt good laying my head down on that pillow knowing I had gotten all my work done. A typical day would be to wake at 6:00 AM, go grab rats by their tail to obtain samples of their vaginal flora for research using that cotton swab, and then attend class off and on until 3:00 or 4:00 PM. I then went to the grocery store to work until about 11:00 PM. I'd grab a snack then head home to study until 2:00 AM or later. I did this for weeks, hated dealing with the rats, but loved the studying. It was a lot of work but extremely fulfilling work (if you like organic chemistry and physics). I was where I wanted to be, and I was passionate about what I wanted to become.

The feelings of accomplishment I had back then came from the structured demands that were placed on me while in college. In grade school you have certain demands placed on you and certain schedules have to be followed. If you follow the schedules and pass the test, you'll get a diploma. We don't have that same structure imposed on us after leaving school unless we create it ourselves (it's called a plan). Now that you're no longer in school, you're responsible for making your own schedule. You must act without needing a teacher or parent prodding you along. You must be your own task master whether you feel like it or not. It's called being self-directed and a grown up.

It's important here to note that we don't necessarily discount our feelings as not having value because many times our feelings help us to make choices in life that are consistent with who we truly are. I'm talking about those feelings that keep you from getting the job done, those feelings that keep you stuck. If you are controlled by negative feelings or depressed moods, it's going to be difficult for you to be consistent in your actions. Negative emotions drain your energy and cause you to not want to do anything. Whether you are running a business or a household you need to be able to act in order to implement any plans you have. Try to recognize your current feelings and determine if they are keeping you from getting from where you are now to where you want to be. If your current state is keeping you from taking action, then you need to think about how you can change those feelings and place yourself in a better mood. The best way to do this is to take positive action.

One of the best ways to change negative, paralyzing feelings and moods is to act in the direction you want to go.

If you don't feel like writing, you should start writing. If you don't feel like exercising, start exercising. If you don't feel like studying, start studying anyway. You'll be surprised how soon your feelings change simply by taking action in the direction you don't currently feel like moving in. In James E. Loehr's book, *Stress for Success*, Loehr talks about the real self and the performer self. The I-don't-feel-like-it self is often your real self, but your performer self is who you are when you act the way you need to act in order to get the job done. The goal is for the performer self to become one with the real self so that you eventually feel like doing what's best for you right now. Loehr talks about how we have to sometimes be actors, acting like we want to do what we are doing, until the feeling comes. We do what's best and eventually feel like doing what's best.

Many people with talent don't reach their goals because they fall prey to what I call the "I don't feel like it syndrome." The question is, when are you going to feel like it, and is it going to be too late once you do feel like it? Stop and weigh the consequences of inaction versus action. Is your inaction moving you closer to your goals? Probably not. Think of those times in school when you didn't study for a test because you didn't feel like studying. Think of how you felt when you got your grade and it was nowhere near as good

Take Action

as it could have been. You felt bad and knew that more effort could have been used to pass the test, but you yielded to your feelings. Don't let this happen. Here are a list of common I-don't-feel-like-it statements. See if you identify with any of them.

I don't feel like exercising.
I don't feel like watching my diet.
I don't feel like—cooking.
　　　　　　　—cleaning.
　　　　　　　—doing the yard.
　　　　　　　—going to work
　　　　　　　—paying the bills.
　　　　　　　—going back to school.
　　　　　　　—starting a business.
　　　　　　　—getting out of bed.
　　　　　　　—[fill in the blank].

The above list has several activities most of us really want to get done but at the onset we don't feel like it. The question is how do we overcome these self-limiting feelings? The most important thing to do is to own up to the fact that you don't feel like doing a particular task. Don't deny the feelings—acknowledge them and then take action. This is having discipline. It's what grown-ups do. Trying to suddenly change your feelings by sitting and waiting is like trying to meditate and stop thoughts from popping into your head. Feelings and thoughts pop up when they want to, and it's up to you to decide what you're going to do about them. The remedy for this is to *take action in spite of your feelings.* You need to feel the feeling and do what you need to do because you know it needs to be done. Just like with courage, you feel the fear and do it anyway. You have to feel the feeling and take action anyway. Of course, this is discipline. You want to start out by trying this a few times until you have confidence that it really works. Taking action works. I make myself write all the time. I don't always feel like writing, but once I sit down and start writing I tend to get into the mood. I work myself into writing. Just think of some task that you know needs to be done, but you simply don't feel like doing it. Now start doing it and see how you feel once you're doing it.

I'm constantly encouraging my patients to walk. Initially, I tell them to just walk fifteen minutes at least five days a week. I also tell them to not worry about how fast they walk, but to just walk. I also warn them ahead of time that they are probably not going to feel like it, but to just do it anyway because I know that fifteen minutes may turn into thirty or even forty-five minutes.

Sometimes we want to take monumental steps rather than starting with a little action and working our way up to larger actions. Choosing too large a goal, such as getting up and walking for an hour when you haven't walked for fifteen minutes in years, sets yourself up for failure. I have set goals so large in the past that the goal was a deterrent from starting because it was to unrealistic. It would be unrealistic for me to write a book in three months especially since I only have a certain amount of time each day to write and this limits the amount of pages I can get done. A more realistic goal would be writing a book in a year. A small step often leads to greater action as you develop the habit of taking action.

You don't take action because you are used to not moving in the direction of your goals. Let's say you've been sedentary, and your New Year's resolution is to join a gym and start exercising. The morning you decide to go to the gym will be difficult because you'll probably be bombarded with feeling tired or you may develop aches and pains you never had before. This occurs all because your body is resisting this change you want to make in your lifestyle. The body resists change, both good and bad because it wants to remain in homeostasis. In George Leonard's book *Mastery*, he calls homeostasis "a condition of equilibrium and resistance to change. " Our bodies utilize homeostasis in a variety of ways. It maintains our blood sugar in a particular range by releasing enough insulin to bring it down if it's too high and to release glucose from glucose stores in the liver when it's too low. An example given by Leonard is the way your home thermostat regulates the temperature in your home. If you set your thermostat on 70 degrees and the temperature in the house goes below 70 degrees, the thermostat will cut off the air conditioning, therefore keeping the room homeostatic at 70 degrees.

We remain sedentary because we've become comfortable not exercising. When we start a new behavior or action such as going to the gym, our body sees this as moving away from homeostasis and

Take Action

therefore creates discomfort. This often translates into I don't like going to the gym, or doing my homework, or reading that report. We can override homeostasis by doing what we should do, realizing that we will initially feel resistance, but after a while we will have reset our thermostat and begun to enjoy the new behavior we started. Some people set their thermostats at 68 degrees in the winter and 78 degrees in the summer. Our bodies tend to adjust to either temperature.

It's tough to get back into an exercise routine after you have stopped, but when you're exercising regularly it doesn't take as much effort to get out and do it. That's because once you're exercising regularly, homeostasis wants you to keep exercising. If I miss too many days exercising I start to miss it and homeostasis is at work trying to get me back in the gym—or walking or running.

Homeostasis doesn't differentiate between what is good or bad for you. We have to decide to act in the direction that's good for us, allowing homeostasis to keep us working in the direction we want to go. Don't be surprised if you occasionally want to backslide into prior lazy behavior. Homeostasis is always at work, and you will always have to battle its effects. I've been trying to slow my writing speed down for years. People think doctors can't write. Well, I'm most doctors, and my chicken scratch can compete with the best of them. Since I've been writing fast and bad for so long it takes great effort for me to write slowly and legibly. It's a habit that homeostasis would have me continue in, but I put in the effort to write better, because it's what I want to happen. I'm constantly met with resistance, but it's a habit that can be broken. We always meet resistance when we try to change a behavior that has become a habit. If you're going to be successful you have to get yourself to develop the habits that will help you become successful. You must remember that resistance to positive change is inevitable. You're not going to feel like changing.

There is a tremendous amount of power in knowing that there is usually some resistance, and often a lot of resistance, to any changes we want to make in our behaviors. Knowing this, don't wait for the resistance to go away before you take action. Take action now. We often procrastinate while waiting for the resistance to go away. The resistance goes away when you decide to take action. If it doesn't go away, then you still have to take action. This is what separates the successful person from the crowd. Waiting for the resistance to go away is an excuse to procrastinate. Even as you begin working you will feel resistance, but successful people work with and through the resistance.

We live in a society that seeks to be comfortable most of the time. Unfortunately, that's not the reality we live in. Anytime you decide to change your current behavior you are usually going to feel as if some force is working to keep you stuck. I feel this all the time. This is why writers who get writer's block learn to start writing anyhow because they know that eventually the block will end. Professional musicians practice for hours every day. They push through the resistance to get their practice sessions in. This can be a daily struggle, but it's a struggle successful people endure all the time. It's what makes them successful.

When acting toward a goal you may reach a point where you want to stop, but in order to grow, you have to drive your way through the obstacles, disappointments, fears, and failures, much like a writer has to write through writer's block. A runner's high doesn't occur after one mile of running. It comes after running several miles. This same natural high can occur when we read, write, study, walk, or study for long periods of time. This high or feeling of accomplishment is earned only through grinding it out with persistent action. Some of my greatest natural highs came when I was in college studying to the point of fatigue and beyond. One reason I decided to go into medicine is because I knew I would have to continue to learn and keep learning as long as I remained in practice.

When I was in network marketing I had to learn a whole new set of skills that expanded my comfort zone. Learning how to do cold calling and presenting products to potential customers was anxiety-provoking but I had to push past the anxiety in order to be a better networker. This, of course, was a good thing. Expanding your comfort zone is always a good thing.

If you don't act toward your goals you will not have peace of mind. You will constantly feel unfulfilled because you aren't doing what you know you need to be doing. This book is at least ten years in the making. I admit to procrastinating most of that time but I had to write this book or constantly feel as if I had unfinished business to take care of. I consider it a gift. All of us were born with certain talents and gifts. We want to use our gifts and talents to help others

Take Action

and get the fulfillment we want and deserve out of life. However, there is a price to pay when we use our talents and gifts. That price is often the uncomfortable feelings we may get when we initially take action. Going from inaction to action disrupts our equilibrium and leads to stress and discomfort. That discomfort is the price we pay when we break out of homeostasis and start working toward our goals. Once one understands this, there is no stopping them from achieving anything they desire. Remember, taking action is initially met with resistance, and this is a natural occurrence. You must break through that resistance if you want to achieve any of your goals. Take action, be vigilant, and have the courage to be the achiever you were created to be.

I don't get bored. Boredom stems from not taking desired actions. When I take time to relax, it is a desired action. You don't have to be constantly doing something because this would take you out of balance. (We need rest and relaxation.) But it's difficult to have peaceful rest if you know that you have unfinished business or you are currently procrastinating. If you think about it, you feel a nagging sensation when you sit around knowing you should be acting on your goals. I think this leads to a depressed mood that could be remedied by simply taking action. It doesn't mean that the goal has to be reached in a day or a week, but it means you are doing something that is moving you closer to your goal.

One thing I've done to help me get my work done is to schedule a block of time. I give myself a designated time to work on a project. If you need to clean out the garage, block out the time to do it. If you need to prepare an agenda, then block out the time for that. I use blocked time to get my writing done. I don't set a goal to write a certain amount of pages or number of words. I simply place my butt in a chair for 90-120 minutes, and during that time I might get one sentence or several pages written but I will be sitting and writing for 90-120 minutes. Toward the end of writing this book I started using thirty minute blocks of times because of my busy schedule. The beauty of blocked time is that it gives you a slot to place your work in. You choose the time that won't interfere with the football game, nail appointment, or soccer practice. With blocked time it's important to focus on the process of what you're doing rather than getting finished. Let being finished take care of its self. If you don't finish it in the allotted time then you block out more time the next day or whenever you desire, but you have to block out the time. The key is to not do anything else during your blocked time except the job you are supposed to do. I can write during my blocked time or sit in my chair staring at the blank page, but I can't do anything else. I can't start paying bills or reading if the time is allotted for writing.

Remember to not place the stress of being finished at a certain time on yourself. This will occur enough in life by outside forces without your placing this burden on yourself. Simply give yourself time to take action. The other thing I think really helps is to give yourself more time than you probably need to reach your goal. If I have to clean out the garage or read a journal article, I am going to give myself more time than needed so that I remove the time pressure. It may only take you thirty minutes to read a report. Why not give yourself sixty minutes so that you don't have to rush and can savor every word on the page. It may only take one hour to clean out the garage, but you could give yourself three hours. Take the time pressure off and allow more than enough time to get the job done.

In many hospital operating rooms there is what's called blocked time. A surgeon will have blocked out 4 hours in the morning on a given day, and that's the time he uses to operate every week. It may be from 8:00 AM until 12:00 noon every Monday. His staff knows that he is in the operating room that day and at that designated time. He will not have scheduled office patients during that time slot. It helps the surgeon and his personnel maintain order and get the necessary work done. The surgeon may not always use all four hours of time, but it's there if needed. You can utilize this same system in your everyday life. Simply block out time to take action and do what you need to do on a regular basis, and you will see tremendous results.

I currently have blocked time every other Wednesday for surgery, and I learned that it's a technique that many writers use to get entire books written. Another name for this method is **time boxing.** I use time boxing for writing, reading, practicing the drums, and doing chores I don't feel like doing. Time boxing may be any length of time you want it to be. I don't give myself a certain amount of work that must get done in my blocked time. I act during this given time frame, and what I don't finish I start back on the next day in another block of time. You can use time boxing to get housework done, write your business plan, or any number of task by setting aside the time. The goal is not to finish but to put in the thirty minutes every day until the job is done or goal is reached. You will be surprised at how much you can get done in just thirty minutes. It only takes thirty minutes a day, five days a week, to stay fit. If you read something thirty minutes a day you would be reading more than a large segment of society. Of course, your blocked time can be as long as you want it to be. It could be from thirty minutes to eight hours. Just make it a realistic time that you can stick to. I've had plenty of practice sitting in a chair watching football so I know I can at least sit at a desk for three hours easily if I chose to.

I don't have a prescription for a magic pill that will make you take action. Even setting aside blocked time requires taking action and discipline. All I can say is grown folks, leaders, and successful people do what they need to do to get the job done. Whining about being tired, or not feeling like it, or the stars aren't lined up just right will not get you closer to your goals. Successful people and people who have decided to take life by the horns take action in spite of fear, fatigue, anxiety, stress, or any number of excuses that other people might use. My prescription for you is to take action and take it now. To do all of the above requires *willpower, discipline, and resolve*.

Chapter Three

Make the Mistakes

You and I are not perfect. I like what Chris Majer says in his book, *The Power to Transform*, in which he states "Perfection is a loser's game—all you can do at it is lose, as nothing and no one is ever perfect, and you aren't going to be the first." Trying to do everything perfectly without making a mistake only sets you up to either constantly procrastinate or not start anything at all. This has been one of my greatest problems.

Whenever I thought about sitting down to write, my inner voice would rise up and start saying things like "you don't have anything to write about or if you do it's not going to be worth reading." I have to remind my inner negative chatterbox that what I write doesn't have to be great or perfect. It just has to be on paper, and then it can be worked on. My writing and practice of medicine are a work in progress, just like you are a constant work in progress. We can work at being better, but we rarely have to be perfect.

Most tasks don't require perfection; they just simply require getting done. Stop worrying about being perfect and start doing. This takes us back to the importance of taking action. We know we need to take action if we are going to reach our goals, but if you constantly worry about your actions being perfectly executed then you won't start anything. It's the problem of paralysis from analysis. If you spend a lot of time thinking about all the things that might go wrong instead of taking action, you don't allow mistakes to unfold. The sooner you make the mistakes the sooner you can self-correct and get the task done.

Again, you have to have courage to be successful. You have to be able to take imperfect actions that could lead to failure and do them with fear and trembling. Yes, you're going to be shaking in your boots, but that's why I emphasize courage so much. You are going to be afraid to make a mistake and that mistake could end up being your greatest insight toward achieving your goals. We've heard about how practice makes perfect, and some have said that perfect practice makes perfect, but the most important instruction I can tell you is that practice requires you to make lots of mistakes and those mistakes are only eliminated by more practice and more mistakes.

I wasn't born a drummer, tennis player, or doctor. I've never delivered a baby that walked to the nursery saying "Hello everybody, I can talk and walk, and I'm only thirty minutes old." Babies don't have egos to get in the way of their learning how to do two very complex tasks—walking and talking. They don't care what they sound like, and they don't care if they fall when trying to walk. This is probably the only time you'll hear me tell you that you need to act like a baby. Babies don't care what they sound like as they learn how to talk. We need to foster that attitude. Stop being concerned with what people are going to think if you make a mistake. None of us are so important that people are focused on us that much. People who see you taking action to reach a worthwhile goal are usually impressed and wish they were doing what they should be doing to reach their own goals. You'll end up motivating them to achieve their goals. I admire people who try and fail yet they keep trying.

"Success is going from failure to failure without loss of enthusiasm."

—Winston Churchill

Make the mistakes. If you embark on any new endeavor you are a beginner. You have to allow yourself to be a beginner. Beginners make mistakes and then learn from those mistakes. I have attempted to learn how to play the piano twice. I usually get through the first lesson book, and then I become impatient and try to progress too fast. This leads to discouragement and then stopping all together. If I simply stuck to it, I would get it done. My problem has been trying to be advanced before my time. I needed to be the beginner for awhile before trying to progress too soon. I needed to pay some more dues before trying to go to the intermediate level. I needed to go through the pains of forgetting certain chords and having to relearn them. When learning a musical instrument you can never play it perfectly without playing it poorly first. It can be frustrating, but the more frustration you learn to handle the stronger you become. Making mistakes and continuing to try is all a part of being a winner.

Baseball players batting .300 means they didn't get a hit two out of three times, yet that .300 batting average can get them into the Baseball Hall of Fame. If you're a baseball or softball player and you can't handle striking out, you probably need to choose another sport. However, any sport or instrument you play will require lots of strike outs and mistakes before you master it.

When I started writing, I wanted every sentence to come out perfectly. I wanted the right words the first time and I wanted them to flow effortlessly onto the page the first time without having to edit them. After reading several books on writing I realized that this was unrealistic. I found out that you have to write a lot of bad stuff sometimes to get to the good stuff. If I couldn't accept the imperfections of a rough draft I would never be able to be a writer. If I worried about writing the perfect book, I would never get a book written.

Procrastination is a by-product of wanting to be perfect. Sometimes I'll decide to simply write junk in order to take the pressure off. You have to admit that it's stressful trying to be perfect all the time and not allowing yourself to just take action, fall, get up, take more action, and enjoy the journey. Being a perfectionist will keep you from moving; perfectionism will keep you stagnant and cause you to procrastinate.

The maxim "Nothing avails but perfection" may be spelled "Paralysis."
— Sir Winston Churchill

Some people like to have the perfect plan before starting a project, so they spend days, weeks, or even months trying to put the perfect plan together. Most of the time they could get by with a well-thought-out outline, with adjustments made as necessary. If your plan fails that simply means you need to revise it rather than whine about how your plan didn't work. You may plan to get up tomorrow at six o'clock to go to the gym, but when six o'clock roles around you hit the snooze button and go right back to sleep. Some people give up at this first attempt to get up rather than trying again the next morning or modifying their plan by gradually waking up earlier over time. We can be impatient with ourselves, not realizing that it takes time to form new habits. You need to allow yourself to fail at getting up a few times until sooner or later you are getting up because you want this new habit to take place. You may have to re-evaluate how you'll be able to wake up earlier. Maybe you'll have to wake up five minutes earlier every morning until after two weeks you're now waking up one hour earlier. Always assess why you don't get up then make adjustments that will help you reach your goal. You may need to simply go to bed earlier. I can tell you from my experience that you are not going to feel like getting out of bed to exercise.

One way to fight perfectionism is to allow yourself to do something poorly. I use this method when trying to be perfect gets in the way of my writing. I give myself permission to write junk. I may just write on the page that "I don't feel like writing today," or "I wish I were playing tennis right now." I remove the goal of being perfect so that something gets written and the habit of writing stays in place. You can do the same thing with exercise. If you don't feel like it that day, then go and stand by the water cooler and watch everybody else working out. You'll at least fulfill the goal of going to the gym, and more than likely you will start feeling like doing a little treadmill work or lifting a few weights. If you don't feel like it, so what, do it anyway. Feelings change with the wind. That's why I know that if I sit down to write junk, I will eventually work my way into writing something worth reading (but not always).

There are times in our lives when what we do need only be a rough draft. We can go back and tweak it later. Simply doing is a great way to conquer procrastination but often our fear of failure or thinking that our desired result won't be achieved often leads to procrastination. Another way to get you moving is to allow yourself to fail. You need to give yourself permission to fail. Beat procrastination by deliberately failing. Practice failing. Get so used to failing that it's no longer a big deal. We tend to get comfortable with certain behaviors that we constantly practice. If you practice failing at nonessential task you'll realize that it's not that big a deal to fail. You'll survive and thrive. The practice will make it easier for you to experience failure in more important matters.

I remember the first year my son played recreational football. Their team didn't win a single game. Most of the boys on the team, however showed up again the next year to play even though they had what the parents felt was a lousy year. I remember thinking to myself how this was a good lesson for the boys since they probably weren't afraid of losing now since they had already experienced losing so many games the year before. They're also more likely to cherish winning in the future and not be so afraid of losing. If there was no chance of losing most of us would not play the game. People like the element of chance. It creates a certain excitement.

Sometimes it's good to do something without placing a desired outcome on the action, but to simply enjoy the actual act for its own sake. When I play golf, I don't care if I win or lose, I'm just glad to be out on the course playing. It's the experience that brings me satisfaction. If I had to play well every time I went out on the golf course I probably wouldn't play. A lot of people rob themselves of the enjoyment of playing a sport or a musical instrument because they don't think they will be able to do it well. Who cares? The world doesn't expect you to be great at everything. Being fulfilled doesn't require greatness. It requires simply doing what you have a desire to do without any stipulations. Sometimes your goal should be to simply do.

It's not a matter of what you can or cannot do, but more a matter of what you are willing to do. I could offer you a million dollars to get up tomorrow at 5:00 AM and go to the gym. Most people would do it because they would be motivated to do it by the million dollars. All of a sudden that I-don't-feel-like-it mood is overcome by seeing that million dollars in your hand.

I have to laugh at the perfectionism I find in myself when I go to the video store. I go in and I look at all the new movies that have been released and some of the older movies, and I can't find a single movie I want to watch. The problem is I can't find a movie that I know will definitely be a great movie. I'm looking for the perfect movie instead of getting a movie for the sake of watching it and letting it surprise me. If it's good that'll be great, but if it's bad at least I will have broadened my experience with movies. Perfectionism places too much emphasis on outcomes. Let the outcome be what

Make The Mistakes

it's going to be. You need to enjoy the process. Let's look at some ways you can practice not being perfect.

1. Choose a task that you know you can't do well and do it badly. An example could be drawing a picture of a person sitting in a chair. Most people if asked to draw anything immediately say that they can't draw. That's why I want you to do it anyway. I want to take the pressure off by giving you permission to draw something terribly just to have the experience of drawing. We often paralyze ourselves by wanting to do things well without ever having been a beginner. Let yourself be bad at something. Try banging on the drums in the music store just for fun. Of course you won't be as good as me at playing the drums. I've been playing since I was in the fourth grade. But that doesn't mean you can't experience the joy of making noise.

2. Do something without any expectation of being good or bad at it. Write a poem. Now I know you think I'm messing with you because writing poetry is felt to be difficult by many, and that's precisely why I want you to write a crappy poem. Don't write a good poem. I want you to write a lousy poem. Nobody has to read it but you. Just do it and see how nice it feels to just do something without it having to be good.

> Roses are red, violets are blue
> Please write this poem for you.

I struggle with writing sometimes because I want to write the perfect sentence the first time instead of a rough draft that can be rewritten over and over until I get it right. As a writer I have to allow myself to write a lot of bad stuff in order to get to the diamonds in the rough.

3. Rent a movie you don't think you'll like. Rent it and then see if you still feel the same way about the movie after watching it. There are some movies I've watched that my wife wanted to see that I felt would be a little girly for me that ended up being enjoyable. I would never have chosen it on my own because it wasn't the *perfect* movie. You can do the same thing with television shows. Watch a show without any

expectation of it being good or bad. Just watch it and allow the experience to unfold without prior judgment.
4. Eat fruits and vegetables for one week. Trust me you will not turn into a pumpkin. See what it's like to be a vegetarian for a week. There's no passing or failing a test here. Just try it and see how you feel. My wife and I did this for a year after we had done a twenty-one day fast with our church. We survived and we learned that there are some very good dishes out there that don't include meat. Try a new dish or fruit that you have never tried before.
5. Take an art class, learn how to play an instrument, or take on a new hobby without telling yourself that you have to be good at any of them. Simply learn for the joy of learning. We've taken a lot of tests in grade school, and because of that we feel as if we are going to be graded every time we learn something new. This adds stress to a learning process that doesn't have to be there. You don't have to ever be on stage playing the piano. You can just play at home and enjoy the experience of playing. So, take the class, keep learning, and enjoy the imperfect ride.

We are products of our educational system. That means we are conditioned to act as if we are being tested or as if there will be a test at the end of a given chore. When we were tested, we either passed the test or we failed. We became conditioned to our actions being judged, and that created a certain stress that led to discomfort and now because we want to avoid the anxiety of pass/fail we may not take action at all. I've taken so many tests to get to where I am that I have definitely been conditioned to think in terms of passing or failing at tasks. We don't have to think this way. We have to train ourselves to take action for the sake of moving in the direction of our goals without thinking about passing or failing. If you pass great, and if you fail that's even better because now you know what doesn't work. Making mistakes and failing can provide a wealth of information if you take the time to review the mistakes and failures. If you fail a test but get with your teacher and go over the problems you didn't get right, you still learned the material. The goal in school is always to be learning and not getting so caught up in the grade. We used to have this saying that C equals MD. In other words, nobody

Make The Mistakes

usually knows if their doctor made all Cs or all As. We used to rely on the C equals MD because we knew that as long as we got that MD we would have accomplished a lot and be allowed to move on to our specialty training. Receiving a C grade didn't have to mean that you didn't learn all the material either. Remember, all we had to do was review what was wrong and then find the right answer.

The beauty of making mistakes is you find out what's wrong and that can often point you in the direction of what's right. Remember Benjamin Franklin had to have a lot of failures before he discovered electricity, but he made it a point to learn from every failure. Remember, failure can point you in the right direction if you take the time to analyze what went wrong. The practice of medicine is not always an exact science, and that's why it's called the practice of medicine because physicians are going to make mistakes. Humans make mistakes and the difference between the successful person and others is that many don't take the time to embrace or own up to the mistakes and learn as much as they can from the mistake.

Think about when you first learned how to drive. Most of us had a fear of parallel parking, but we kept practicing this skill until we got it right. You probably practiced parallel parking over and over again until you could do it reasonably well. You were willing to practice this skill again and again because you wanted your driver's license. More than anything in the world you wanted that license, so you were willing to practice, fail, practice some more and keep failing until you got it down well enough to go take your test. When we want something bad enough we will put up with the mistakes and learn from them until we reach our goal. It's just like the toddler learning how to walk. Falling down and getting back up is life. Remember, you learned how to walk and talk. Those are not small feats. You have to allow yourself to be that little toddler again who keeps getting up and trying over and over again until you succeed.

Practicing is what you're doing when you are making mistakes, learning from those mistakes, and working toward your goals. Give yourself permission to make mistakes and fail, because that's what successful people do.

Chapter Four

Practice

It's a funny thing, the more I practice the luckier I get.
—Arnold Palmer

You have to practice. Practice is another one of those most important elements needed for you to be successful. People achieve greatness because they practice being better at what they do, and they practice a lot. In Andre Agassi's autobiography, *OPEN*, he talks about hitting 2500 tennis balls a day as a child. He eventually became the number one tennis player in the world, and I'm sure the amount of time he put into practicing helped him achieve that goal. All elite athletes, musicians, and artist practice for hours in order to get better at their craft. They practice with an intensity that's called deliberate practice.

Deliberate practice requires focus. The elite performers are totally immersed in what they are practicing such that they can only practice for about five hours at most a day and even then it's broken up into short segments lasting only sixty to ninety minutes. They often repeat the same movements over and over again until they get it down so well that it's second nature to them. This type of practice can be used in all disciplines. If you have to give a speech, you practice giving that speech over and over until you feel comfortable. Whatever you do as a profession or trade you will do it better if you practice doing it.

If you are a manager, executive officer, or speaker you can practice certain skills to make yourself better. No one is automatically good at something. Yes, there are some people who have a talent for

Practice

singing, math, writing, or a particular sport, but they don't become good and especially not great by not doing it over and over again. You will have to work on your skills. It doesn't just come. You'll have to train and train and work and strive and sweat and stretch yourself on an almost daily basis to be great. It takes consistent practice.

According to Geoff Colvin in his book, *Talent is Overrated*, he says "Top performers repeat their practice activities to stultifying extent." If you want to be a good piano player you need to play the piano a lot. You have to sit and practice for 60-90 minutes, take a 10 minute brake then resume playing for another 60-90 minutes. Ninety minutes is the length of time most people can focus intently on a given subject, and often the limiting time is 60 minutes. Top musicians usually practice for up to 5 hours a day broken up into an hour to hour and a half segments.

It's not usually fun to practice for long periods of time. It's a battle with yourself. You will constantly have to use self-motivation to do what you do. I play music while I write because I love music and I have to motivate myself to sit down and write. So I listen to music to help get me up to the task of writing. It keeps my brain stimulated. Steven King listens to rock when he writes, and he would write for four hours at a time, every morning, even on holidays. That's what I call being in the game. If you want to be great at something you have to do it a lot. If it's writing, you write a lot; if it's music, you play a lot. The same goes for all disciplines. You have to practice a lot of hours to get better.

You also have to read about how to get better, or better still find yourself a coach who can guide you and make sure you are practicing the proper techniques. I could go to the driving range every day and hit golf ball after golf ball and not improve much because I wouldn't know what to correct my swing. Top performers almost always have a coach to show them what they need to do to improve. A coach shows them what they may be doing wrong so that it can be corrected. Every Olympic athlete has a coach. Every professional musician has had a teacher or coach help them to get to the status of greatness. Tiger Woods and Andre Agassi had their dads to initially coach them, and then they had professional coaches in their respective fields coach them. It's important to have someone look at what you're trying to do and correct any weaknesses you might have.

Whatever you might be doing there is probably an organization that you can turn to that can help you find coaching and support. As a physician, we have to go to conferences for continuing medical education, and if there is a new procedure to learn we find someone who is already good at the procedure and have them assist us until we become proficient enough to do the procedure. It's also good to read about people who are at the level of expertise that you want to reach. Read the biographies and autobiographies of high achievers. This will give you an idea of how they practice, and you will see the dedication needed to become great.

I have to warn you, focused practice (deliberate practice) isn't much fun. Your desire to be better must constantly override your desire to not practice. The hardest thing to do is work on a weakness. When I played tennis as a kid it was easier to keep practicing my backhand because it was my more stable stroke. It was more painstaking to work on my forehand because it was the shot that needed the most work. Remember, if you want to be great, you have to work on your weaknesses. You work on your weaknesses until they become one of your strengths. This is something you will need to do if you aspire to greatness.

Again, this isn't just for athletes and musicians. Chess players, writers, pilots, speakers, teachers, and a host of other professions require you to do deliberate practice if greatness is to be achieved.

You also must allow yourself to be a beginner. We tend to want to be better than we can realistically be without having put any effort into doing anything. I'm sure that at some time in your life you have thought about learning to play a musical instrument, or take up art, or learn to play tennis, only to have that little voice in your head tell you "Who do you think you are? You can't play tennis, or draw, or play that instrument." Well, of course you can't, and you shouldn't be able to because you have never done it before. That's why you take lessons. That's why we have teachers. That's why you are a beginner. Hey, if we want to stimulate the economy we need to start putting the art, music, dance, and sports instructors to work teaching us how to do new things. Allow yourself to be a beginner, then eventually you can become proficient, good, great, and who knows, you might even start teaching the same skill that you learned to somebody else. But you have to allow yourself to be a freshman, a starter, a beginner.

Practice

Guess what? Beginners have to make mistakes, and lots of them. That's why you have practice sessions so that you can make mistakes, learn from them, make more mistakes, then learn some more from those mistakes. As a writer, my initial draft has all kinds of misspelled words, and grammatical errors. The second draft has some also, but as I continue to write and rewrite, I eventually have a readable piece of work. I allow myself to put something on the page, even if it's junk. Sometimes out of junk comes a golden piece of writing, but I can't get to the gold without rummaging through the garage sale in my head. Let yourself be the worse tennis player on the planet. Draw the ugliest stick figure in the world. Go to the music store and buy a harmonica or small flute and play some bad music. If you think you can't sing, just listen to me someday and you'll have lots of hope. You'll easily sound better than I do when I sing in church.

We often think that an audience is watching us try to do something that we've never done before. We act as if there is an audience waiting to criticize our every move, and tell us that we're not the next *American Idol*, or that we're going home after an audition. Well, most of us aren't the next idol, but we can at least grow and expand who we are by doing new things, taking on new dreams, maybe writing songs for the next American Idol, or coaching the next future sports star. You have to ignore the chatterbox in your head that says you can't do this or do that. Often, you have to *just do* and let the results take care of themselves. Let yourself enjoy the process.

They say perfect practice is needed to become good at anything and I agree with that, but you won't get to perfect practice until you simply practice, find out how you can be better, then practice some more. You learn to practice what's right and do that over and over. *It's not easy.* Most of the time it's not fun, and the only reason you're practicing is because you're so focused on what you're doing that you're not thinking about how much you don't feel like doing what you're doing. This is an important point. The successful person practices more than the average player. We talked about the elite musician who practices four to five hours a day. You have the great basketball players like Larry Bird and Michael Jordan who practiced their sport more than their peers. They loved the game and they practiced their sport more than the average professional player. Andre Agassi wasn't in love with tennis, but because he practiced so much and trained extremely hard he was able to be the number one player in the world. There's no telling how many more titles Agassi would have won if he had loved the game. This just goes to show that a ton of deliberate practice with analysis of the mistakes you make leads to success. But you have to allow yourself to not be perfect. You have to allow yourself to make the mistakes and keep on going.

You will always have to practice. I wish I could have reached a level of proficiency at tennis and then been able to stop and continue to play well but life doesn't work that way. To continue to be good at what you do, you will have to continue to practice. There will always be another speech, another player waiting to beat you, and another executive wanting to be CEO. This isn't a bad thing. We don't grow as human beings by staying in our comfort zones. Life demands continual effort on our part. We have to keep weeding the garden if we want it to stay clean. That's how practice works. If you don't continue to practice, the weeds come back and bad habits sneak their way in. Remember, the best performers in the world still have to practice almost every day to remain proficient at what they do. There is nothing special about any of us that we won't also have to practice, practice, and practice some more in order to be good and stay good at what we do.

Practicing your trade is one of the prices you'll have to pay if you want to be good and especially great at what you do. There are no short cuts to success. I repeat ... *there are no short cuts to success*. Success demands a price. You have to be willing to pay that price. People usually see the finished product. They see the rock band on stage and the beautiful groupies around them, but they don't see the hours of practice that went into playing the instrument, or the many gigs they played for free at a friend's party. People don't realize how many one night concerts in small towns that they played for just enough money to buy a hamburger and gas and enough to make it to the next hole-in-the-wall place to play until 3:00 AM. People see Tiger Woods hit moon-striking drives into the middle of the fairway, but don't realize that he had to hit thousands of balls to be able to drive the ball with such accuracy and distance. It's inspiring for me to see Olympic athletes perform because I know it takes a tremendous amount of practice to make the Olympic team, and if you place gold, silver, or bronze you are the three best at what you do in the

Practice

world at that moment. Imagine being the three best of anything in the world. What a feeling. Now think about what it would feel like to be up at five in the morning practicing for two hours before work and then another two hours after work. Think about how tough it is to do that remembering that that's often what it takes to be one of the best. You may not be preparing for the Olympics, but you may be preparing to advance in your company.

It's one thing to know what it takes to be proficient. Most of us may understand how to do something, but to be able to do it requires a tremendous amount of effort and many are not willing to put in the effort. Your success is always going to be tied to your persistent concentrated practice and your ability to practice whether you feel like it or not. I've talked about feelings in this book and how you must learn to act often in spite of those feelings. You won't feel like practicing a lot of the time, but practicing during these times is what will separate you from the crowd.

Malcolm Gladwell's book, *Outliers,* has a chapter that goes in debt regarding the amount of time a professional practices verses the amateur. The amateur pianist and violinist from childhood to age twenty practiced on average about two thousand hours, while the professional would have practiced ten thousand hours. That's an extra eight thousand hours. Ten thousand hours is the equivalent of ten years of practice, Monday thru Friday, for three to almost four hours. You have to pay a lot of dues to get to the top of any profession, and that payment is in hours of practice and study. Knowing this and accepting this is a major step in the direction toward your success. Proficiency will only come from practice and any attempt to get better without practice is an exercise in futility.

You have to make practice a habit—something you know you will do because it has become something you do. You almost don't have to decide whether you are going to do it or not because it is a part of you to do it like brushing your teeth before going to bed or as soon as you get up in the morning. If there is an area in your life that needs to be worked on you need to practice in that area with focused concentration until it becomes second nature to you. An example would be learning how to play tennis. The first habit you would need to begin is simply going to the instructor and taking lessons regularly. If you had lessons every Saturday at 9:00 AM then your next habit would be to show up for that lesson every Saturday. The next habit would be to get used to holding your tennis racket a certain way as instructed by your coach. The next habit would be to learn how to swing the racket and watch the ball. You would continue to add habits that would eventually help you to become a good tennis player.

Every time we take on a new endeavor we have to practice at that endeavor until we improve. This is where we have to allow ourselves to be beginners. Think of yourself as that little baby crawling on the floor. Are you still crawling, of course not? You decided as a small child that you wanted to walk and you decided to deal with falling down several times in order to be able to learn to walk. We forget about how much practice it took for us to walk and talk. We think too much. We're so grown up now that we can't allow ourselves to fall or stumble. We worry about what people think rather than focusing on being everything we could be. Be a beginner, fall down, stumble and laugh at yourself as you try to play that guitar or piano or get those words on paper or write that poem, start that business, or go back to school. Get in there and start practicing as a beginner. Success is often simply starting something new, enjoying the task, and practicing it because you like doing it. Play golf because you like being active outside. Write a poem because you want to write a poem and don't judge it as good or bad. Just write the poem. Nobody has to read it but you. Your fifth grade teacher won't be grading it.

Most of us have been so conditioned by our scholastic upbringing, having been subject to twelve years of grades that we feel like we are being graded every time we do something. Remember, you are no longer in school. There are lots of things you need to do just because you enjoy doing it, not because you do it well. We make life harder than it needs to be because we tend to make our activities one of pass/fail. We also spend a lot of our time worrying about failing. Just do what you like to do over and over and over and allow yourself to get better at what you do. As stated earlier, it's okay to be a beginner at something you have never done before. Every great performer started as a beginner, practiced their rear ends off, failed a lot, but eventually reached their goals. Therefore, make practicing whatever you want to achieve an integral part of your life.

Chapter Five

Courage

Courage is the ladder on which all other virtues mount.
—Clare Boothe Luce

I'm scared. I live with fear every day. I have performed caesarean sections for over twenty years and I still fear the process. I believe this to be one of the most important chapters you will ever read because it will help you to move with your fear to reach whatever goals you might have now and in the future. You may be *afraid* that you've picked up a book that is not going to help you. I want to help save you the time of waiting for fear to go away and help you to realize that fear is going to be your constant companion in this world and that courage needs to become your best friend.

When I was a teenager I played tennis almost every day. I wanted to be the next Arthur Ashe. I would practice in ninety-degree heat all day, and because of my diligence I was good enough to receive a tennis scholarship for college. I looked great in practice, but I had one big problem. I choked when I played against opponents as good as or better than me. Choking in sports is when you allow your nerves or fears to get in the way of your performance. It can cause a tennis player to not hit the ball hard for fear of hitting the ball out of bounds. It can cause a basketball player to miss a free throw when the game is on the line, or a golfer to miss a two-foot putt she would normally make ninety-nine out of a hundred times. We all have our choking moments, but the successful business man, athlete, or performer learns to reduce this tendency to choke under pressure in order to be the best at what they do. I want you to come away from this chapter knowing that you are not the only one scared. It's alright to be scared, but don't let being scared keep you from taking the necessary actions needed to reach your goals.

Courage is taking action in spite of your fears. It is taking action when you are scared and your hands are shaking and your stomach's churning. I'm scared every time I perform a caesarean section, not because I don't know the technique but because I have a scalpel in my hand and one of the risk factors associated with performing a caesarean section is cutting the baby when entering the uterus. No obstetrician wants to have to tell a mother that her infant has a cut on their face caused by the procedure. A physician's fear often stems from a strong desire to do no harm. My greatest fear in the operating room stems from my desire to do no harm to my patients. Your fear might be speaking in front of a crowd. I doubt you are afraid of the crowd. You're mainly afraid of not giving a good speech, looking silly, or people staring at you. I've never had an audience rush the podium to attack me while I'm speaking. Our fear of speaking is the fear of messing up, or of looking foolish. Yes I'm scared, fearful, and anxious every time I speak, but this is a good thing. It means I care about the quality of what I am doing. You're scared because you want to do well, and you are afraid you won't deliver. Remember, you will have the fear of speaking for the rest of your life as long as you care about putting forth your best effort. Fear is going to accompany you on every speech or performance, but you need to bring courage along with you.

Life is scary, don't let it fool you. Courage is a best friend. Don't ever leave her.

When I was in elementary school we had to take gymnastics. You may remember the parallel bars, horse, and the different floor exercises that come along with gymnastics. I hated gymnastics because I was afraid of getting hurt. I never could do a cartwheel mainly because I was afraid I would fall on my butt. Falling and I don't get along. I admire gymnasts who grab hold of those fears and hug courage so tightly that they can toss themselves in the air and land on the mat without stumbling. Are they anxious, of course, but courage is their trusted friend. Gymnasts have also fallen many times, but they get up and keep practicing because they develop the courage to do so.

If we live our lives trying to avoid anything that might lead to fear, we are essentially trying to escape life. I've read several books dealing with fear, and I tried to find a book that would help me eliminate fear once and for all. I was desperately looking for the magic ingredient that could rid me of that uncomfortable feeling of fear. I read Susan Jeffers's book, *Feel the Fear and Do It Anyway*. A great book, but I didn't want to *feel* any fear. So I kept searching. I read quotes about fear, and none of the books or the quotes told me what I wanted to hear. I wanted somebody, anybody, to tell me how to get rid of fear. No one was cooperating, and the reason why was because you cannot get rid of fear.

You Cannot Get Rid of FEAR.

You Cannot Get Rid of Fear

You may perform a task so often that you are not afraid of doing that particular task any longer, but if you try doing a new task fear raises it's big head again. I have performed hundreds of circumcisions and have no fear of cutting the tip off the penis (this has happened before—not by me, thank God and knock on wood). However, this is one of the primary fears residents have (rightly so) when I teach them how to perform a circumcision. Now, I admit that I do have the fear of them making a mistake while I'm teaching them. I'm scared, anxious, and afraid because I am not the person with the scalpel, they are, and even though I have never had a problem performing the procedure and none of my residents have made any mistakes while performing the procedure, I am fearful of that possibility. This fear is a good thing. It gives me a heightened awareness and reminds me that this minor procedure can have major consequences if a mistake is made. You can never be too careful when performing a circumcision, and I constantly want my residents to remember this. Again, my fear is out of my concern for and desire for a good outcome. Fear helps you to keep your guard up, but it must not be allowed to paralyze you. A speaker may be comfortable talking to an audience of one hundred people but then become nauseous and fearful when asked to speak before one thousand people.

I admire the military and law enforcement for what they do every day to protect us. They, along with firefighters, have to constantly deal with fear in order to do their jobs. There are few fears greater than being at risk of losing your life or limb in the line of duty, but these men and women do it every day. Fear is their constant companion, yet it's courage that befriends them and makes them do what must be done to assure our safety.

A hero embraces courage at the moment just prior to the action that will end up defining them as a hero. Think of the 9/11 heroes who rushed into the burning Twin Towers. They were scared yet they knew that this was that defining moment when all their training would need to be put into play and they had to act in spite of their fears. You may not have to run into a burning building, or dodge bullets any time soon, but you may need to muster up the courage to take on more responsibility at work, ask for a raise, speak before your peers, or apply for that new job or position.

Think back on some of the lost opportunities you had because you let fear get in the way. We can't grow without courage. Personal growth takes us out of our comfort zones and fear will stare you down if you let it, because you are venturing into uncharted territory. Like the explorers Lewis and Clark you're going into uncharted territory, at least by you, and you will be scared. Medical school was one of the most rewarding four years of my life. It was also four of the most stressful years of my life. I lived in constant fear of failing, fear of harming a patient, fear of presenting patients to my professors; fear of not having tuition, and on and on. But in spite of these fears, I had to do what needed to be done in order to get my medical degree. Again, I had to feel the fear and do it anyway, and that's what having courage is all about. If you're working on your MD, PhD, master's degree, RN, Technical degree, BS, or GED, just know that it's alright to be scared. You're in good company. You don't focus on the fear; you take appropriate action while you hold hands with fear. It's not easy for the successful person, and it won't be easy for you.

You gain strength, courage, and confidence by every experience in which you really stop to look fear in the face. You must do the thing which you think you cannot do.
—Eleanor Roosevelt

Do you remember the first time you did anything of significance and the amount of courage it took for you to do it? You were afraid, but you didn't allow that fear to stop you from taking action. Your desire to achieve your goal was strong enough to make you act in spite of your fear.

When I was admitted to medical school, I was both excited and scared. I was excited because I wanted to be a physician, and now the opportunity was there, but scared because of the challenges that lay before me. Would I be smart enough to grasp all the information I had to digest? What if I flunked out of medical school? What would my family and friends think? I had all of these fears, but at the same time I had this strong desire to be a doctor. Desire is a strong motivator that often invites courage along for the ride and pushes fear over to the side. I'll talk about desire later, but it's true that my desire to be a doctor had to outweigh my fears of failure. Now that I am a physician I *still* get scared, frightened, and anxious. I have to make decisions every day regarding whether I'm going to take action in spite of fear or allow the mere presence of fear to control me and squash my plans. I wish I could say that I'm fearless but I'm not.

Fear can interfere with your plans for success and prevent you from persevering when you need to push on to achieve your goals. Fear of success occurs because we often fear the responsibilities that accompany success. The employee who works hard and now is up for a promotion becomes anxious because the managerial position she worked to get carries added responsibilities. Take the example of Susan who is currently executive vice president at her firm. She has thought about what it would be like to be president of the company. She goes to leadership conferences each year to help her grow and become a better leader. Her department is outperforming all the others, and there's a rumor that the current president is thinking about stepping down. She would become one of the top candidates for the position. Susan knows she is qualified for the job, but she is anxious because it carries more responsibilities. She is accustomed to her current responsibilities so there isn't as much anxiety in performing her duties, but now she could be asked to be in charge of the company. This is a position Susan wants and has developed herself to have, but she is scared. She is scared of what this success will bring her. Her relationship with other vice presidents in the company might change. Is she ready for the responsibility? Does she know enough? Is she ready in spite of all the leadership conferences and books on leadership she has read? Susan is afraid of failure and success. If offered the position she will need to confront those fears.

In this situation, Susan could let fear keep her from being president of the company. If she decides not to take the position, this could be detrimental to the company since she is the most qualified for the job. Can you identify with Susan? You may not be up for president of the company, but it could be a new skill you won't try because you've never done that before, and you're afraid to try for fear of failure, yet learning that new skill could help advance your career or increase your income. There are certain procedures I do all the time—caesarean sections, abdominal hysterectomies, tubal sterilizations to name a few. But there are some procedures that I did not do in my residency training such as total laparoscopic hysterectomies using robotics. There aren't many gynecologists trained to use the robot to perform gynecologic procedures at this writing, and part of that is because the robot is not in most hospitals and many physicians have not been trained to use the robot yet. Since I decided to learn how to use the robot, I again had to deal with the stress of learning something new and have the courage to learn the new procedure in spite of my fears of harming the patient, or simply failing.

You may have been asked to help coach little league baseball, or recreational football or basketball. Will you let fear keep you from sharing your talents with young people hungry to learn how to do what you already know how to do? The world has been robbed of many gifts because of fear.

Dr. Benjamin Carson is one of my chosen mentors, even though he doesn't know it. He is a world-renowned pediatric neurosurgeon at John Hopkins Hospital, Baltimore, Maryland. He performed the first successful separation of twins joined at the back of their heads. He also pioneered the hemispherectomy to help eliminate and reduce persistent seizures in children. Was there fear involved? I'm sure there were many anxious moments, and there was a lot of doubt by many regarding whether such a surgery could or should be done. Just think of the many children that have been helped because Dr. Carson looked fear in the eyes and said "let's do it." His book *Take the Risk*, talks about dealing with and taking calculated risk—risk that requires courage.

If you want to develop courage, start reading everything you can get your hands on that deals with courage. Read about courageous people. Read about people you look up to that exhibit the characteristics you want to have. Allow courageous people to speak into your life. We tend to act the way our peers do. Well, guess what, you can choose your peers. I chose courageous people like Dr. Carson, Gandhi, Colin Powell, Dr. Martin Luther King, Mother Teresa, Navy Seals, Army Rangers, Theodore Roosevelt, and Dr. Benjamin E. Mays, to name a few. You may know some or all of these heroes, but the bottom line is you can choose to read and know about courageous people. Let them rub off on you. Everyone could use people in their life that motivate them to be more than who they are right now. Think about how television and radio advertising influences our purchasing decisions. Just think of how much better off you would be if you made a conscious decision to feed yourself words from the great thinkers of yesterday and today. It will rub off on you. You'll start to think and act like your chosen peer group.

Courage is the first of the human qualities because it is the quality which guarantees all the others.

—Sir Winston Churchill

I love the above quote by Winston Churchill because it is so true. Think about trying to do the right thing and how we are often afraid of what people will think. It takes courage to make a stand and say I don't do that anymore. I give high praise to patients who tell me they have been drug-free or sober for months or years because I know it took courage to stop and courage to stay away from the drugs and alcohol. We are often afraid to discipline ourselves to stop a bad habit because we are afraid of failure. We give up dieting because of past failed attempts at losing the weight so once again we allow fear of failure to get in the way of our success at losing weight. It takes courage to keep trying and failing, but that's what it takes to reach any goal. You have to keep working at it daily. Every day try to be courageous. If you fail today, try again tomorrow.

When I was on the tennis team in high school we use to hit one shot over and over until it became second nature. If I had to work on my cross-court forehand, I would hit cross-court forehands for an hour every day. Initially the shots would go in the net or out of bounds. That didn't matter because we knew that eventually we would be able to consistently hit the ball in bounds. It didn't happen after one or two attempts but only after hundreds of tennis balls had been hit. It takes courage to stick to something until the goal is reached, and this goes for anything you're trying to achieve. To act in spite of our fear of failure or success is to act with courage. If this is an area you feel is a problem for you, then make it your study.

If you are having problems dealing with fear and lack courage, I suggest you read everything you can get your hands on that will encourage you to have courage every day. The reason I say you need to make a study of courage is because we as people tend to get excited about changing and act courageously for a brief period then fall back into our old habit of shying away from challenges. You want having courage to become a habit. Focus on being courageous for the next six months to a year and see how life changes for you. I have to recommit myself to acting courageously every day. Read biographies about people you admire, and if you get a chance, go talk to or get around people who you admire that exemplify the characteristics that you want to exhibit. Read a biography on Winston Churchill or Gandhi or Dr. Martin Luther King. You may choose to read about people in your field of work who did or are doing heroic things. I chose Dr. Ben Carson because he's a physician. You want to choose people who you can relate to if possible. Choose people who are at the top of their fields.

You could go to seminars where you can talk directly with people who are taking action in spite of their fears and who can give you advice. When I was in network marketing, I went to conventions and seminars that helped me to deal with the fear of cold calling and presenting information in front of people. I received a lot of information either in tape form or live from people like Mark Victor Hansen, Les Brown, Zig Ziglar, Jeffrey Coombs, Jim Rohn, and the list goes on and on. My library is a Who's Who in the self-help arena.

Constantly exposing yourself to positive people and their books is what it takes to keep pushing yourself to the next level.

I mentioned cold calling above, and I have to say that cold calling people to talk about a product is as scary as public speaking to me. It takes courage to be a good salesperson. You have to make the calls you need to make or risk not making the sell because you are afraid of the phone.

I used to make cold calls and I was shaking in my seat when I initially started but, after doing it a while and realizing that no one was going to come through the phone and get me, it started to get easier. Getting past the initial fear is the biggest hurdle, and that's where you have to decide if you want the results bad enough to have the courage to make the call. There are lots of gimmicks and mind tricks we could play to get ourselves to act but I think the most important thing to remember is that you have to *act with fear*. If acting with fear becomes a habit then you will be equipped to do great things.

Writing is a scary business. Ralph Keyes book *The Courage To Write* is one of the best books I have found on dealing with the fear of writing. I think it's a great book for anyone struggling with fear because the information carries over into all areas of creativity and life. Consider this passage by Keyes:

"Trying to deny, avoid, numb, or eradicate the fear of writing is neither possible nor desirable. Anxiety is not only an inevitable part of the writing process but a necessary part. If you're not scared, you're not writing."

I venture to say that if you're not scared you're not living as boldly as you could be. You're not going after that promotion or new job. You're not taking that class to learn how to play an instrument or draw dance, or play tennis. Anytime you embark on a new venture you are going to be anxious and that's normal.

Successful people are scared and courageous.

When I was in the fourth grade I decided I wanted to play the drums. At that time the elementary school I attended offered music lessons, and I decided to take them. It was fun because I had always enjoyed beating on magazines and anything else that made noise. I was in the band from elementary school throughout high school.

During that time I had a lot of performance anxiety. I had the anxiety of playing in front of my instructors and eventually playing in front of crowds of people. I played all the way through my senior year in high school. I've played in parades and in concerts, but with every performance there was anxiety, stress, tension, and fear. Fear of making a mistake, or the fear of looking silly in front of the audience. I was one of the best in the state of Maryland in my day but that didn't keep me from being scared every time I performed. If I had allowed fear to get in the way of my playing the drums, I would have not had as rich a childhood and been able to enjoy the wonderful people in music that you always meet when you are a musician. *Being afraid is often the price you'll pay to enjoy life to the fullest.*

I repeated the same pattern when I learned how to play tennis. There was always the stress of winning and losing. Performance anxiety was always there and is still there when I play a tennis match now. It will never go away. I've read book after book trying to find one that would tell me how to get rid of fear. Bottom line, there is no getting rid of fear. We are never alone. Fear is going to be a constant companion with us. The sooner you accept that it's not going anywhere and like Susan Jeffers says "feel the fear and do it anyway," the more living you'll get to do. If you want to be a better parent, employee, soldier, leader, or anything else it will take plenty of courage.

It's not easy. It's a challenge for anyone who is still breathing air. Fear can make you nauseous, shake, vomit, urinate, and yes it can cause some to crap in their pants. I can't eat anything just before speaking, and I always go to the restroom before any performance. Your intestines like to get into the game whenever you decide to do something that challenges you. Maybe that's where "intestinal fortitude" comes from. Our intestines like to get into the act when we're nervous, but we have to have the guts (pun intended) to still take action.

Every area of our lives requires courage: the courage to be married and stay married, to raise children, to change careers, and to simply learn something new. It takes courage to live.

Sometimes even to live is an act of courage.
— Marcus Annaeus Seneca

If we look at any given week of life we've lived, we can note fear standing on all sides. We have had to make decisions regarding our fears. We can spend a lot of time trying to eradicate fear but, as I said earlier, this is usually futile since the fear of one action is usually replaced by the fear of something else. You can decide not to write, learn new things, or explore new places; however, you would miss out on many of life's riches simply because of fear's paralyzing effect on you. We must take the risk which is paramount to having courage. We have to risk being embarrassed, talked about, ostracized, or ridiculed, if we want to achieve the success we deserve. Again, it takes courage, and having courage will have to become a habit. Habits take time to develop, but the habit of having courage is one of the most important habits to cultivate since it will allow you to develop all other positive habits and traits that you want to have. I will be discussing that through the rest of this book.

Courage is the greatest of all the virtues. Because if you haven't courage, you may not have an opportunity to use any of the others.
— Samuel Johnson

Let's take a moment to digest the above quote by taking a human quality such as loving others and see how this quality is helped by courage. If you are to love your neighbor as yourself you may do well as long as your neighbor looks like you do, has the same religion, votes in the same party, and admires you. If your neighbor doesn't like you, doesn't vote, and is from another ethnic group you may have some discomfort loving this person because you feel like you are giving of yourself and they might not care about you. We lack courage if we allow fear to prevent us from exhibiting love toward those who we think may not respond in kind. Love takes courage because it must be done in spite of the fear that it may not be returned. This is one of the great lessons I've learned over the years: I have to have courage to love people. I can't be afraid that they won't return the love to me. I must be man enough to love others in spite of what others feel about me. Unconditional love requires consistent courage. Commitment, persistence, discipline, and integrity require courage. Developing a plan and sticking to it requires courage. Again, it takes courage to live, and everything I suggest you do in this book will require you to have the courage to take action and do what it takes to be the success you can be.

Chapter Six

Plan to Succeed

Planning is something all of us tend to put off because we just don't like to plan. Much like flossing our teeth every day, planning is what we should do but often don't feel like doing. I don't like to plan, but I know that it's necessary to be successful. If you have no plan, you're essentially planning to fail. You've probably heard that statement before, and it's an accurate statement. It's hard to travel from Atlanta, Georgia, to Los Angeles, California, for the first time without using a map. That's what a plan does for us. A plan is your map to your goal.

We often don't plan out of our fear of not keeping to our plans. If you had the confidence to stay with your plan, you probably would keep to the plan. You have to have faith that the plan you set up will help you achieve your goal. Have you ever planned on getting up to exercise the next morning, but when the next day came you stayed in the bed? Maybe you were supposed to start that new diet of fruits and vegetables but found yourself stuffing fried chicken wings down your throat instead. You planned on calling your parents to see how they're doing but just didn't seem to get around to it. If you have enough of these failures to implement your plans, you'll begin to think that you just don't follow plans; therefore, why make a plan? I've done all of the above, and I always regretted not following through. Trust me, following through feels much better than not following through.

One big mistake we make is going about our plans in a linear fashion—step one, step two, and so on. I want you to try simply writing down all of the tasks you need to get done in order to reach your goal. After that simply pick a task and get to work on it. Let's say you plan to go back to school to get a degree in business. You would write down all the different action steps you would need to take on a sheet of paper such as choosing which school, getting applications, arranging your current work schedule, figuring out how to finance this goal, and on and on. After you have written all this information down, you pick one task and do it. Don't get stuck on trying to figure out which one to do first, second, or third. Just jump in on one task on your list and get busy. We allow ourselves to procrastinate when we spend too much time trying to organize our plan into this perfect sequence of tasks. Obviously you need to decide which school you would apply to first before getting applications, but you may choose several schools, and it won't hurt to get the applications from all the schools you choose. The goal is to put your plan on paper and then start working it out without stressing over the order of things. Pick a task and start working on it.

Some plans are already established for us. When you're in high school the plan is laid out for you. Finish high school and you get a diploma. That's the plan. If you don't stay in the plan, you don't get the diploma. One of the reasons some of us stayed in school is out of fear of our parents. We didn't want to disappoint them, and we also knew that having a diploma is a good start to getting a job. There is often both negative and positive reinforcement associated with the plan of finishing school. Our parents are usually the ones providing the motivation. As we get older and have other goals, we don't always have anyone but ourselves to motivate us. Your parents are not going to call you every day and ask if you have started working on your goals. You will need to be self-motivated. Self-motivation is important when you are trying to reach any goal.

One of the major problems I've had in making my plans is not incorporating any fun or leisure in the plan. You are going to have to put some rewards in your plan to help keep yourself motivated. If you only plan to work, you don't give yourself anything to look forward to. I'm good at planning to read journal articles or self-help books and doing household chores, but I need to work harder at scheduling time to play golf, go fishing, or go to the movies. If you're a hard-working individual, you probably don't have a problem planning to work because you know that no work equals not getting your bills paid or not eating. We sacrifice certain pleasures in life because we just don't plan to play as often as we did when we were children. When we were kids we had the entire weekend scheduled with fun things to do. We often didn't have anything planned. Remember when Friday came and everyone in your high school class wanted to know what was happening that night. I remember planning to just have fun, fun, and more fun. Where is the party? We need to do the same now, but be balanced in our planning. If I plan on writing for three to four hours, then I also plan to do something that I really consider to be enjoyable. Writing is fulfilling, but it is work and it can be hard work. Make sure you have balance in your planning. Plan to work, plan to play, and plan to sometimes just do nothing.

Discipline, persistence, and faith are needed to work a plan. You need to make yourself design a plan for success, persist at it, and have faith that your plan will help you reach your goal.

Now faith is being sure of what we hope for and certain of what we do not see.

—Heb.11:1

When you have faith, you are confident that your plans will lead to success. You act, knowing that your actions are not in vain. There's a certain amount of anxiety associated with having faith, but you can't let that anxiety get in the way of you carrying out your plans. Be afraid, but don't let the fear put a damper on your faith. Work your plan.

By the way, it's okay to change plans or modify your plans. Sometimes the direction you want to go in has obstacles that you should go around rather than plow through. Your original plan may have been to plunge ahead, but that would have taken too much time. So you go around the obstacle instead and reach your goal in less time. When I was in high school I played on the tennis team. I would practice on the backboard for hours, but there were times when my arms would get tired and I would have to stop practicing earlier than I desired. If I didn't stop practicing, my form would get sloppy and I would stop benefiting from the practice session. There was a point where continuing to practice yielded diminishing returns. I had to decide whether to continue practicing that additional hour as planned or stop and be satisfied with my accomplishments for the day. You'll constantly have to make decisions regarding whether to stay the course, modify it, or abandon it altogether. Either way, the experience often leads to personal growth.

Why don't we stick to our plans? It's usually because of a lack of discipline. A lack of discipline can keep you from making a plan because deep down we know we're not going to stick to it. The only way to break this habit is to follow through with our plans. Just do it. To have success you have to be able to tell yourself what you want done and then have the discipline to do it. If you fail you fail, but at least you'll be able to look yourself in the mirror and say you tried to do it. At least you will have given yourself an opportunity to learn something by working the plan. As stated in the chapter on discipline, you can't afford to wait until you feel like working your plan. You have to work the plan, and let your feelings follow your actions.

Sometimes we have plans, but it's all in our heads. It's best to get it out of your head and onto a piece of paper. Goals are more likely to be reached if written down. Write your plan out on a piece of paper. This helps reduce mental confusion and foster better organization. These days there seems to be so much information to keep tract of that it's easy to let important things slip through the cracks. Write it down. Keep a record of what you want to do or be. It will help you to see where you've been and where you're going. Remember, this doesn't have to be in linear fashion. Just write down what needs to be done, pick a task, and go to work. Constantly taking action toward your goals is how you reach your goals.

I planned on being a professional tennis player when I was growing up, but that plan had to be changed after I started playing college tennis. I realized I wasn't anywhere near as good as I needed to be to compete on that level. I had to fall back on one of my earlier aspirations to be a physician. It's important to remember that just because you fail to reach a particular goal doesn't mean your plan was in vain. The discipline and dedication you applied to that previous goal will often be needed in carrying out future plans and achieving new goals. The hard work and training I put into tennis carried over into my medical school training. Running every day, hitting that tennis ball against the backboard hundreds of times and losing tennis matches helped to mold me into who I am now.

Plan To Succeed

A failed plan just might be your ticket to success in another area. There's nothing like failing your way to success.

Sometimes you have to fail just so you can know who you are, what you want in life and whether you should continue in a certain direction or not. The fact that you've failed at planning before is no excuse for not planning. Failed plans make for successful plans, so plan to be a success. Don't leave it to chance, and don't complicate it. Sometimes my planning is simply writing down what I want to do for that particular day. After I write it down, I then decide whether I need to prioritize my list or not. You don't have to always prioritize your list. Sometimes you just need to get all the stuff out of your head. If you see that there are certain tasks that need to be done first then do them first. Just don't make planning so complicated that you don't want to do it. I love to KISS (keep it simple, silly).

Planning takes effort. That's why you'll often hear people say that they don't plan to do anything on their vacation or their day off. And that's okay. It's not good for you to have every waking hour planned, but you must have appropriate balance in your life. That balance usually leans toward more work than play, but that's the way we were designed. The core nature of people is to work at something that gives them fulfillment. It's important to learn to work hard but also to play hard and often. When I say work hard I 'm talking about being totally into what you are doing—giving it your all so you can enjoy the harvest of a job well done. I have to say that there are going to be lots of jobs we don't feel like doing, but the finished results give us tremendous satisfaction. That satisfaction doesn't occur however without doing the work.

Make sure you plan time to simply have fun. Plan to do something you like to do when you're not working. I love to read when I'm not delivering babies or seeing patients. Some background music, plus a book, and my life is good. A little golf here, a movie there, and I'm ready to get back to work. Make sure you treat yourself to time off doing what you like to do. Remember, you need to plan to work, play, and do nothing. That's what it takes.

You don't have to have a perfect plan. You can spend a lot of time trying to create the perfect plan and end up procrastinating because of planning. Get the steps you need out of your head and on paper. Start working on one of those steps as soon as possible. Try to do something every day that moves you closer to your goal, and don't wait until you feel like it. Take action now, and know that your plan is subject to change several times as you move toward your goals. As you learn more and reach certain milestones along the way you'll find that something you thought needed to be done one way will now have to be done differently. That's good because it means that you will get the task done more efficiently—or you may find out that you didn't have to do the task at all. You may be thinking that you need to do ABC and D, but with increased knowledge and insight you only need to perform A, B, and D. Having a plan allows you to know where to start, restart, stop, regroup, and sometimes rethink the direction you might be going in.

Think of how you might plan to use a navigational tool to get you from where you are to your home address. If the tool gives you a route that takes you longer than you know it should you are likely to pull out a map or go the way you already know. You won't keep going in a direction that is counterproductive, just like you wouldn't continue in a plan that you see is not moving you in the right direction. You constantly need to make corrections that will move you toward your goals. Remember, there are no perfect plans. Your plan might be putting everything you know needs to be done on a piece of paper and then choose one thing and get to work on it. Once you get that one thing done you need to start the next one that you feel needs to be done. Don't be linear; choose an action that is on your list whether it is the next item or not. Your goal is to finish the list, but you often don't have to complete the tasks in any particular order.

Probably the most important thing you do will be writing down your goals and the actions you'll need to take to reach those goals. You have possibly heard this many times before, but it warrants repeating: written goals are more likely to be achieved than none written ones. So write your goals down, make a plan to accomplish those goals, and don't try to be perfect about it.

Chapter Seven

It's Hard

One of the best chapters I've ever read was written by Hal Urban in his book *Life's Greatest Lessons*. The title of the chapter was "Life Is Hard . . . and Not Always Fair". It hit home with me at the time because I had been struggling with the current state of medicine with increased malpractice claims and decreased reimbursements for services. I was also having a tough time getting myself to sit down and write this book. Looking back on my life, I had lost my mother after childbirth, my brother to suicide, and a marriage through divorce. I had experienced corporate bankruptcy and was currently being sued for medical malpractice. Yes, life is hard.

It's hard, but when events occur in your life that are bad, you can't roll over and play dead. It's tempting to, but you have to accept it and keep moving in the direction you need to go. If you roll over and play dead or give up, life will continue to roll over you. When you've got kids to feed, rent to pay, and a job to do, you can't afford to sit around whining about how tough life is. Kids want food, landlords want rent, and bosses want people to show up. Nobody wants to hear excuses. Life doesn't care about our excuses. Life wants to see what you are made of. I wish bad things didn't have to happen, but unfortunately they do and we have to get up and keep going.

Sometimes life is hard because of the resistance we often feel when we decide to do something. Have you ever noticed that as soon as you decide you're going to do something constructive, this weight of resistance seems to kick in? It doesn't have to be something we don't like to do either. When I decided I wanted to write a book there were so many obstacles that presented themselves. These obstacles were not physical but mental. One of the biggest obstacles was not feeling like writing. Others were fatigue, doubts about my ability to write, and doubts about whether anyone would want to read what I had written. If I had continued to think this way, I would never have gotten around to writing this book. It has also taken longer than it should have because this world likes to see how bad you want something. I think all of us have our doubts about our abilities to perform in an area we're concerned about. There's a certain amount of resistance we feel whenever we decide to do something constructive. Think of the resistance you feel when you decide to get up early and exercise. It's almost as if there's this anti-exercise monster pushing us away from the treadmill. I reached a point where I was tired of that resistance keeping me from doing what I wanted to do. I was tired of fatigue being an excuse for not getting a task done. I was tired of using the excuse that it's too hard.

Life is hard because sometimes we have to give up sleep and still be able to get the job done. There is a certain amount of resistance that we feel when we don't feel like doing something. If you don't feel like doing it, that's a good indicator that it probably needs to be done. This is especially true if we want to do the task but just don't feel like it.

We tend to want to feel good all the time, but that isn't the reality we were born into. I strongly agree with what Hal Urban said in his book, "The world will not devote itself to making us happy." I wish it did but it doesn't. Life will kick you in the seat of your pants, tell you to get up, then kick you again as you try to get up. Life is hard. Life is also suffering according to the first of the four noble truths written by Buddha. "Life is difficult," as stated by psychiatrist M. Scott Peck in his excellent book *The Road Less Traveled*. The above truths need to be digested after being chewed on over and over again. A reminder of this truth needs to be placed in a conspicuous place so as not to be forgotten. Large numbers of people keep looking for easy ways out or quick ways to success.

Most people who are looking to lose weight are looking for an easy way to do it. Patients want a pill to take because that would be the easy way to lose weight. Unfortunately, exercise and proper diet are what people need to lose weight. Yes it's hard to lose weight, and the sooner one accepts that it's hard, the better. People remain miserable or disenchanted with life because they're looking for a world that doesn't exist. Easy street doesn't exist, and our fairy godmothers retired before they even started working. I wish, I wish, I wish it were not so, but it is.

The challenges of life are what make life worth living. We were created to tackle problems. This is how we grow as humans. Life constantly stretches us if we'll let it, but you have to let it. Life also continues with or without you. If you don't get on board, life will keep right on going, and if you get in the way it will trample all over you. You need to jump into life and play to win. I like to play games to win as most of us do, but imagine what it would be like to always win easily. There would be no sport or challenge to the game anymore. We need challenges, and deep down within us we want a challenging and interesting life. The great highs of life come at the expense of hard work and solving problems. One could also say that life is full of problems, and it's up to us to solve them until death do us part.

Difficulties exist to be surmounted.
—Ralph Waldo Emerson

A residency in obstetrics and gynecology is tough because of the lack of sleep and the stress of taking care of both a mother and her unborn child. I was up all night many times during my residency, and we all learned to function tired and make decisions under stress. It was hard, and I remember thinking about how much easier it was going to be in private practice. Well, guess what? It's still hard and stressful. Most physicians learn to simply deal with it. If you don't, you end up fighting reality—the reality that practicing medicine is often stressful, fatiguing, and difficult. But, so is raising children, doing a nine-to-five with only two weeks' vacation, looking for a job, working your job, and living this life. Learn to accept life's difficulties. When we continue to fight certain realities, we find ourselves feeling discouraged, because we're looking for a life that will never exist.

Bottom line, life is hard because you have to press on in spite of your feelings, fatigue, doubts, fears, or anything else that might be used as an excuse to quit or not even start. You have to be a warrior. Whether you're a housewife running a home or a CEO of a major corporation, you will meet with resistance and need to make a decision regarding whether that resistance is going to stop you or stimulate you to plow through and reach the goals you desire. Successful people take the resistance they feel and turn it into a stimulus for action. If it sounds like it might be hard to do, successful people see it as an opportunity to do something many others aren't willing to do. A lot of people who think about becoming physicians could if they just decided to pay the price. It's not that they don't have the mind for medicine; they just don't want to put in the hard time to achieve that particular goal. For me it was thirteen more years of education beyond high school. That's a lot of dues to pay, and it was hard. But if you want to be successful, you have to do the hard stuff that others are not willing to do.

Deep down within ourselves we like certain goals to be hard to reach. We want our lives to have some challenge to them. These challenges, however, can be stressful. During residency, other physicians who had been practicing medicine for years were around to teach and guide me through different difficult situations that came up in the hospital. When I got into private practice I made major decisions, and the responsibility fell squarely on me. I have to be prepared to deal with a dying patient, stillborn infants, and miscarriages. A mother at childbirth can lose a lot of blood quickly, and situations can go from good to bad in a heartbeat—especially if it's a fetal heart beat. There's plenty of heat in an obstetrician's kitchen, folks. Do I get out or do I stay in. I stay in realizing that certain stresses and challenges come with the territory. Is it hard to be an obstetrician? I think it is. It's very hard to get up at 3:00 AM when you have already delivered six babies, and you had just laid your head down on the pillow, and the emergency room calls to tell you that you have a patient with an ectopic pregnancy about to go into shock. You now have to be up another two to three hours operating on this patient who just placed her life in your hands. It's now 6:00 AM, you haven't slept in twenty-four hours, and Mrs. Anybody just showed up fully dilated and ready to push. Once again, I have to rise to the occasion and do what I'm trained to do—work tired and under stress. Is it hard? Yes it's hard. There were times when I was nauseous because of the fatigue. It's hard, but it's probably why obstetricians do what they do. There is fulfillment in doing hard things.

Don't let fatigue prevent you from reaching your goals. I fight fatigue on a regular basis even if I've had my eight hours of sleep.

It's Hard

Being tired when we're working on something makes what we're doing seem harder than it really is. Also, if you really want to make life hard on yourself, start out tired. This is why it's so important to get enough sleep. We'll discuss getting enough sleep later, but just know that lack of sleep is guaranteed to make your work harder to do.

It's important to occasionally ask yourself if you're making life harder than it needs to be. I could be justified in complaining that I have to get up at 3:00 AM to deliver babies, but I have to remind myself of the rewards I get from being who I am. I work in air conditioning in the summer, heat in the winter, and I get to eat plenty of good food. My salary is excellent and since I've been delivering for over fifteen years there are certain events that don't stress me as much any longer. My most frequent adverse condition now is being tired and working through negative feelings. We have to constantly reevaluate our life circumstances, and when we do we may find that it's not as hard as we thought or as hard as it could be. Make sure you keep things in perspective. I hate traffic, but it sure beats walking.

Try to think of what usually keeps you from doing what you want to do. What makes your life hard? For me it's the fatigue factor and the stress of not feeling like doing something. Let's talk about the fatigue factor. When you're tired, it seems as if your body is working against you. The spirit is willing, but our physical nature is not. Life seems harder when you have to make yourself do what you want to do in spite of the fatigue and in spite of how you feel. Winning the battle against fatigue is key to success and separates you from the average person. It's good to practice doing a task that you don't feel like doing just to see how it feels to do that task. Try walking for thirty minutes even though you don't feel like walking, just to see how it feels to be a walker. Trust me, you won't explode if you make yourself walk for twenty to thirty minutes. It might be hard for you to do if you haven't done any significant walking in years, but of course, life is hard. You'll probably find that walking is not as hard as you think, and you might even start to enjoy it. We have the habit of not giving ourselves a chance to be better by using the excuse that the effort to perform a task is too hard.

The ultimate measure of a man is not where he stands in moments of comfort and convenience, but where he stands at times of challenge and controversy.
— Martin Luther King, Jr.

God sells us all things at the price of labor.
— Leonardo da Vinci

I've come to a place in my life now that I can say without question that life is hard more often than not. It was hard work getting a diploma, BS, MD, complete a residency, and remain in private practice. It's hard work just getting out of bed sometimes. We work hard. We will always work hard, and the trick is to accept this fact and learn to live in the knowledge of this fact. Character development occurs when we take on the challenges of life. Some of those challenges are placed on us against our will, but we still have to dig in and do what has to be done. We tend to come to grips with our current existence and figure out ways to deal with it once we accept that life is the way it is. Think about those people who are born blind, deaf, or without a limb. They learn to deal with their situation and often times live lives with more gusto than many people with all their faculties.

Once we accept that life is hard, we can begin to take the necessary steps to deal with the difficulties and hardships that cross our paths. Unfortunately, some of us try to escape the hardships of life by either turning to drugs, alcohol, or some other vice that can lead to self-destruction. Some people get depressed because they want life to magically get better without doing anything differently. We're bored because we're not doing anything, but we're not doing anything because it's so hard. We keep waiting for things to not be hard; consequently, we don't get anything done of significance. If I had waited for medical school to become easy I would have had to give up my desire to become a physician.

When you're in your last two years of medical school, you rotate through five core areas of medicine—psychiatry, obstetrics and gynecology, general surgery, pediatrics, and internal medicine. I remember when I did my rotation in internal medicine; the room was freezing and I was terrified of the chairman of the department.

It's Hard

He would ask questions about the patients we had rounded on that morning. I was always afraid of not knowing the right answer and getting embarrassed in front of my classmates and the family practice residents. That was three of the most miserable months of my life. Being nervous and cold at the same time is a bad combination. It was hard, but not unbearable.

Sometimes we call something hard because we've never done it before. I'm a doctor of medicine, but I don't know anything about fixing a car, planting a garden, making lasagna, or any number of other tasks that I haven't been trained or taught to do. I could say fixing a car or planting a garden is hard, but the mechanic and gardener probably view them as being challenging but not necessarily hard. It's not that it's hard; it's that we don't have the knowledge needed to perform the task. We can either complain about how hard it is to fix a car because of our lack of knowledge, or we can hire somebody to fix the car. The other option is to learn how to fix the car. A little knowledge can remove a lot of hardships.

The stress and anxiety associated with thinking about how hard something is can be worse than the stress and anxiety associated with performing the act. The act of doing releases a lot of stress. The first time I delivered a baby in medical school, the anxiety felt prior to doing the delivery was greater than what I felt while delivering the baby. Patients who have minor procedures in the office are usually anxious about the procedure, but once it's over they usually state that it wasn't that bad and they don't know why they worried so much about it. Some patients worry because they talk to friends and family who seem to always tell them the worst possible thing that could happen. Then the patient worries her head off right up until the procedure is over. Some patients postpone their surgery because Aunt Somebody's brother-in-law's cousin knew a lady in Peoria who never played chess again after her hysterectomy. We can become so focused on the one percent chance that something bad is going to happen that we sacrifice our ninety-nine percent chance for success.

He that forecasts all perils will never sail the sea.
— Anonymous

We make certain tasks hard by thinking about all the things we need to do to accomplish the goal. If your goal is to become a computer programmer, you shouldn't think about all the classes you'll need to take. Just focus on one class at a time. Tackle one semester at a time, and the next thing you know you have a college degree. Two of my colleagues obtained their law degrees while practicing medicine at the same time. Think about it. One night they might be up delivering a baby, and the next night they're up studying law. And let's not forget they still had to see patients during the day. Was it hard? Of course it was. But if you want something bad enough you'll do what you have to do.

The next time you hear yourself calling something hard to do I want you to ask yourself these questions?

1. Do you really want that which you're calling hard?
2. Why do you consider it to be hard?
3. Will it still be difficult to achieve if you break it up into small pieces?
4. Is there something else more worthwhile you could be doing other than what you've decided is too hard?
5. Is there just as much or more stress thinking about doing it as there is doing it?

Let's examine each of the above questions. First do you want that which you're calling hard bad enough? We often say we want something done but only in words. When it comes down to doing the work we find out we really didn't want it as bad as we thought. It's like seeing a nice suit, wanting to buy it, checking the price, and then deciding it's not that good because the price was too high for our taste. The high price that comes with reaching certain goals changes a lot of people's minds about going after that particular goal. However, sometimes we don't care how much the suit cost; we want the dress because we think it's worth the price. Is your goal worth the price and are you willing to pay it? If you want it bad enough you'll pay the price no matter what.

The second question of equal importance is why do you consider the task to be hard? When we choose a goal to reach, its common to think about all the needed steps we'll have to do to reach the goal.

It's Hard

We begin to think about our current lack of knowledge regarding how to reach a particular goal. We create a monster out of the task by trying to know everything at once. We make a goal seem difficult to reach by assuming we have to know everything about how to reach the goal before we even start. We make the goal hard to achieve or consider it to be hard because our minds get cluttered with to-do lists that should be written out and not simply held in our heads.

Let's say you want to go to college and become an architect. You might start thinking about all the courses you'll need to take, how you're going to get to school, how you will afford it, and what if you can't do it. You may start to think about how long it will take, and you may know someone who tried to become an architect but failed. These can all be legitimate concerns, but we allow all of these concerns to hit our brains all at once. We get so overwhelmed that the next thing we know we've labeled something too hard to achieve. When I decided to go to medical school I had all the typical concerns. What if I don't get in, how will I pay for it, and will I be smart enough to stay in once admitted. It's best to write your concerns down. Get them written down and out of your head. Then chip away at each concern one by one. Make life easier by taking it in small bits rather than large chunks at a time. This answers the third question. Will the task still be difficult to achieve if you break it up into small pieces? Let's just say it's easier to dig one hole at a time, especially if you only have one shovel.

Is there something else more worthwhile you should be doing other than what you're calling hard? Let's see, should we write a book or watch another episode of a played out television show, stare into space, or complete that application to graduate school? Maybe we should sleep one more hour rather than walk thirty minutes. We have to make choices everyday between actions that are pleasurable but may not have much value nor contribute to helping you reach your goals. I used to like watching television and have put in as many hours as the best of them, but I have to say the fulfillment I get from reading a good book or getting a necessary job done around the house far outweighs the television. If you have a goal you're trying to reach, you probably want to assess the amount of time you devote to watching television versus working on your goals. This leads me into the next question. Is there just as much stress or more thinking about taking action versus going ahead and doing what you need to do?

It's hard for me to enjoy television if I know I should be finishing a project. Things start to bug me and goals start screaming at me when I procrastinate. The discomfort of inaction forces me to act. Take the time to examine how you spend your time. Days, weeks, and years go by quickly, and some of our dreams and aspirations may end up going to the grave with us. Many will never live up to their potential because they're waiting for life to get easier. Well, I wish I could direct you to a self-help book that could give you an easier way, but of the many I've read there is no easy success. The daily grind of life is hard, and it's made harder by not accepting this fact. If something comes easy for you, thank God. If life seems hard and appears to be trying to beat you down, thank God. Life is still good, it's just hard too.

Chapter Eight

Develop Good Habits

People who are successful have developed habits that lead to success. They get up early because it's a habit. They exercise regularly because it's a habit. They work hard because they have developed the habit of working hard. Once you develop a habit you start to do things automatically and it becomes awkward when you act contrary to the habit. This is one of the benefits of a good habit. I recently started to play more tennis because I had fewer hospital calls and I needed the exercise. Because I had developed the habit of hitting forehands and backhands with a certain amount of form as a teenager I now have the ability to hit the ball well. This form was developed from hours and hours of practice thirty-five years ago. We won't talk about my golf game, however.

You can continue in bad habits, or you can develop good habits. A person can smoke, do drugs, and drink too much out of habit, or they can read, eat healthy, and exercise out of habit. It's all up to you which habits you want to develop. It's hard to break certain habits but like Les Brown says, "sometimes you have to do it hard." Once you have developed the habit of exercising you'll tend to miss doing it if a few days go by. Instead of craving a cigarette you could exchange that desire for a healthy habit such as exercise.

It's been said that it takes twenty-one days to develop a habit and that may be true for a habit you've only had for a brief period, but if you have had a habit for twenty years it will take you much longer to break. Our habits become part of our subconscious, and often we don't realize a behavior has become a habit. Our conscious mind must re-train our subconscious mind, and this takes effort. It requires discipline and perseverance.

When I played tennis in high school, I had the habit of getting up at six in the morning. One of my friends would pick me up, and we would go to the YMCA's indoor courts and practice for an hour before school. After school I would go back to the YMCA to practice or I had team practice at school. I didn't think this was anything difficult at the time because I loved playing tennis and it became a habit. Practicing and playing tennis for hours was a habit that helped me to become very good at the sport. It initially took conscious effort for me to get up earlier, but once I did it for several mornings it became second nature or a habit to do. It became routine.

When you watch a professional tennis player hit a forehand winner down the line, it's usually done without any thought regarding technique because it's now a habit that the player developed from hours of consciously trying to hit that particular shot over and over again. Once you are in a match where you need to be thinking strategy and you also have the stress of losing or winning, you can't afford to use up mental energy thinking about how to hit a particular shot. You have to be able to make shots without thinking about them. Habits allow you to do things automatically. This is when you are in flow. You don't have to spend time thinking about what your next shot is going to be. When you get in the habit of waking up at five o'clock to exercise, it becomes routine and less of a struggle. Notice that I said less of a struggle. This takes conscious effort, and taking conscious effort requires work.

The good thing is that good habits, once developed, are hard to break just like bad habits. Think of an action that you know would make you successful in your job or profession if you did it all the time. What if you developed the habit of reading in your field at least one hour a day? What kind of difference would that make in your life and work? You could become one of the top performers in your field. What if you developed the habit of exercising thirty minutes a day? Think of how good you would feel, and the weight you could lose if you were in the habit of eating mostly fruits and vegetables. Think of what it would be like to not have to think about whether you were going to exercise, eat healthy, or read one hour a day. You just did it because you were in the habit of doing it. Well, successful people develop those kinds of habits that lead to success. It's like the person who is in the habit of investing at least fifteen percent of their income for twenty years. They now have a nest egg that they can retire on because of the simple habit of saving a little bit of their money over a given time period. You want to take the time to decide what you could do on a regular basis that would make you more successful. Once you decide what that is, you then put a ton of effort into making that behavior a habit. It will take a ton of effort too. Trust me, it's difficult to change a behavior that's been with you a while. I've been trying to slow down for years, and I've come to realize that it takes constant vigilance for me to slow down and take my time. I have only been able to do it by constantly reminding myself of the benefits of slowing down. I have the desire and I have a "why" for slowing down, and those two reasons motivate me to work at it daily.

Develop the habit of working hard—working hard at those jobs that will make you successful. Think about how much you could get done if you developed the habit of throwing yourself wholeheartedly into your work. You plan and you execute your plan diligently without wondering whether you are going to follow through or not. You want to develop a confidence in yourself that doesn't doubt whether you will follow through with what you set out to do. This is power. Developing the habit of making a plan and following through with that plan is guaranteed to lead to success. There should be no question regarding whether you are going to do what you say you are going to do.

Getting in the habit of working and realizing the fulfillment associated with working will catapult you to a whole new level of human. This is especially powerful when you incorporate a plan and goals. Knowing that you will work your plan out of habit gives you an edge over the average person. That average person who doesn't realize their potential.

The great thing about school is that it tends to impose certain habits on you. When I was in high school band we had band class for fifty minutes at least three to four times a week and because we had regular performance tests, it forced me to practice on a regular basis. This obviously led to the habit of practicing my instrument regularly and leading to my success as an "All State" drummer. Schools create habits for us while we're there but once we are out "in the real world" we need to discipline ourselves to take action and form our own success habits. We become grownups who have to tell ourselves what to do.

It's not easy, but if you were looking for easy you wouldn't still be reading this book. You want results, and results don't come easy. However, if you can take a task that is difficult and do it enough times such that it becomes a habit, then you will eventually meet with great success. You have to grind it out. I am in the habit of waking up in the middle of the night and driving to the hospital to deliver babies. All obstetricians are able to do this. We would prefer all deliveries to be from nine to five but that's not nature's way so we have been conditioned from residency to function in the middle of the night and to make tough decisions when we may have just awakened. These are habits laid down from residency. It's habit, but it can still be difficult. As stated earlier, life is hard. Habits, however, can help.

Bad habits, lead to bad results. Procrastinating is a habit, and it can be overcome by getting in the habit of taking action immediately. I know that sounds simplistic and it is. You will need to make a decision every single day to take action immediately and not procrastinate. You will have to consciously make yourself develop this habit, and you will have to protect this habit with all your might. You will need to get into the habit of protecting your good habits and not falling into bad habits. I cannot overemphasize that this is a lifelong journey. Just like the lifestyle most people have to undergo when they change diets or exercise, you have to make focusing on maintaining good habits a lifetime discipline. This will require you to consciously analyze where you are in your life and what you are doing on a daily basis. You need to determine if what you are doing is taking you closer to where you want to be. Will you be successful if you continue to act the way you're acting now, with the habits you currently exhibit?

Remember, to fight procrastination you have to not give your brain time to talk yourself out of taking action.

Remember, people judge you by the habits you display on a daily basis. Are you constantly late, lazy, unmotivated, and undependable? If that's what they see by watching you daily, then you are going to have to work on developing more positive habits that people can know you by. Wouldn't it be great if you were known for being very health-conscious because people see you exercising regularly and eating nutritious foods? It would be nice to be known

Develop Good Habits

for being well read and a person that takes charge of a situation and gets the job done. These behaviors can be yours with constant practice. It takes work as stated before, but that's why you won't be the average person. You can be the person that industries seek out or that gets the promotions.

I like to work. I watched my parents go to work when I was a child and I noticed that all the men and women in my family worked, so I figured that work must be an integral part of life. I started out cutting grass at about age twelve, and then in high school I worked for McDonalds. In college I worked as a resident assistant for a year, then after changing colleges I worked at a grocery store to pay for a car and my tuition. I know all about working. It's a habit that I plan on having in place until I die. I like to work. I like playing the drums, playing tennis, and reading. Those disciplines come much more naturally to me than writing, however. I have had to make writing a habit because it's an arduous task on days when you don't feel like sitting in one spot and writing. Because it's a habit, I now feel worse about not writing than I do about sitting and writing. I have read book after book on writing, trying to find a book that would tell me how to write a book without pain and suffering. Unfortunately, there is no such book out there, just a lot of very good writers telling me through their books that I need to simply sit my butt in a chair and write. I especially love the statement that writer's write. So, I have had to develop the habit of writing. I decided that I needed to do something regarding my writing every day. I can't afford to not write everyday because I want this habit to remain until I retire from writing.

Brian Tracy wrote a wonderful book called "Eat That Frog." It talks about dealing with procrastination. The frog represents the task that you put off or that you absolutely don't feel like doing but you know you need to do in order to be successful. If you were to eat a frog before you did anything else, anything else you ate the rest of the day would be minor compared to eating that frog. Tackling your most important but difficult task first thing in the morning would set you up to handle many other minor tasks throughout the day. Try to get in the habit of doing your most difficult yet most important task first and do this every day. Take the time to figure out what three major tasks you could do on a daily basis that if done would lead to monumental success for you. After you pick those three tasks see if you can narrow it down to one or two. Those one or two tasks must be done every day. You must make yourself do those projects or tasks no matter how you feel. As a matter of fact, the most important of tasks must be done regardless of how you feel. I repeat ... *you must do it every day*. If you make this a habit you will meet with great success and begin to develop a self-confidence that helps you tackle other important challenges in your life. Remember, you will not feel like it.

Some people choose exercise as their most challenging task, and therefore do it first thing in the morning. That way there are no excuses later in the day about being too tired or not having enough time. When you accomplish a major task at the very beginning of your day it gives you a sense of accomplishment. That feeling of accomplishment carries a person throughout the day. When I go to the gym to work out prior to going to the office, it gives me a since of accomplishment early in the day. It jump-starts my day. Now I exercise after work by playing tennis or walking. My most important everyday job now is writing. I have to write every day. I don't feel like it, but I want to do it because I have information I want people to know and that I feel will benefit them. I also write everyday because it maintains the habit of writing. I feel uncomfortable if I don't write every day, even when the words are hard to come by. I brush my teeth every day, bathe every day, read every day, and there probably are other things that I do out of habit that I don't think about. You have the power to consciously create an outstanding life for yourself by developing habits that lead to an outstanding life.

It's hard, it's hard, it's hard, but it's worthwhile. I'm going to say it again, it's hard, it's hard, and it's hard. Making yourself do anything that is challenging and takes you out of your comfort zone is hard. We're scared and concerned about failing, but neither fear nor chance of failure prevents the successful person from achieving their goals. I have often not started a task in the past because I was afraid of failure. You may be afraid to start a new habit even though it will be a habit that changes your life for the better. The good news is that you get to mess up a lot when you are establishing a new habit. Don't expect to start a habit without some challenge to your consistency. You will miss a day or two, or seven. You will have doubts regarding whether what you are doing will benefit you. You will be scared, but that only means that you are an achiever. You are someone who is taking charge of their success and not waiting for luck or chance to somehow get you through life. You are not a dreamer but a doer. As I've stated before, you have to do what you have to do if you want to be successful and that means establishing successful habits.

When I was in medical school, I, like all of my class mates, had to study all the time. We would be up at all times of the night looking at pathology slides or reading. We fell asleep in our books, and drank more caffeine than any human should. I used to stand up to read because I would have fallen asleep if I sat in a chair. I would stand a while, and then sit a while. I would do whatever I could to stay awake. Listening to music helped. I had a classmate who could watch television and study at the same time. All of the above were habits that were used to help us sleep-deprived students make it through medical school.

Again, these were habits forced into place by school. When I was in college I made it on four hours of sleep. I would go to work at the grocery store from 5 o'clock until 11:00 PM after which I went home and studied until 2:00 AM. I would get up at 6:00 AM to go feed the lab rats prior to getting to class at 8 o'clock. It was a habit. Yes, I would fall asleep in class, but I already knew the work because I had studied it at 1 o'clock the night before. I don't recommend living on four hours of sleep on a regular basis but there are times in life when you find yourself needing to do what you have to do to get the job done. It's habit that will make the difference. I look back on some of the work I did back in college and medical school and wonder how I did it, but it was all a matter of having developed certain habits that lead to success.

Here are some habits that I know lead to success:

1. Reading at least one hour a day in your field.
2. Exercising thirty minutes at least five days a week.
3. Eating mostly fruits and vegetables.
4. Tackling your most important task first thing in the morning.
5. The habit of discipline.
6. Setting goals and writing them down.
7. Reading to develop yourself.

8. Plan your day the night before.
9. Take action immediately; don't procrastinate.
10. Being grateful for what you have.

You don't have to try to develop all of the above habits at one time because each one requires a tremendous amount of effort. Try to establish one at a time. The beauty of taking on one habit at a time is that your success will be enhanced, and accomplishing one habit will help you to have confidence that you can develop more habits that will contribute to your success. Simply choosing that habit that will impact your life the most and developing it will be life-changing. If you develop that one major habit, it acts as a stepping stone to your ability to developing other important habits. You have probably heard this before but it takes about twenty-one days to develop a habit. It may take even longer. But just think of the number of good habits you could develop over a year. Yes, you could have seventeen new success habits. Take exercise as an example. When you make a conscious effort to exercise regularly, you start to feel better about yourself and have more confidence in yourself. This confidence will spill over into other areas of your life.

Don't forget, none of this is easy on anyone. We all have to struggle to develop good habits. It's hard to break a habit and it's hard to establish new success habits, but just think of the rewards of doing it. Remember, if it were easy, everybody would be doing it. Everybody would be slim and trim. Everyone would be working toward the career they wanted and most of us would be eating healthy and reading a book a month.

If you make your most difficult job a habit, it becomes less of a burden. Your feelings will have to fall in place with what you have decided to do with your life right now. We talked about feelings and taking action in an earlier chapter and developing success habits is another way to put your feelings in their place. Not feeling like establishing a habit that will take you to the next level is no excuse. You have to establish success habits, or you will be tossed all over the place emotionally. To be consistently happy in this life, you have to consistently do what you want to do, and it's habits that will help you do that.

If you want to be a strong CEO for your company, you will need to read about CEOs of great companies and what characteristics they

Develop Good Habits

possess that you need to develop. If you're going to be a professional musician you will need to study what it took the top musicians in the world to be who they are. If you want to be successful, you have to start doing what successful people do and continue to do to be successful. It's all about the success habits that they perform every day. There are no shortcuts, magic pills, or fairy godmothers that will make you successful. Working hard and establishing success habits is what it takes to be a success.

Chapter Nine

Slow Down

Slow and steady wins the race.
—The Hare and the Tortoise

Success takes time. If you want to be successful, you should try slowing down. We're moving too fast in our world of computers, e-mail, faxes, planes, trains, and automobiles. Remember, you're a human, not a machine. We've created things to move fast for us. Give yourself time to do what you need to do and enjoy doing it. Savor the moments. Remember, technology should enhance our enjoyment of life, not create more stress in it. Our handheld computers should help us save time by keeping us organized and on schedule, yet we end up overbooking ourselves. Housewives have dishwashers, washing machines, garbage disposals, automatic coffee makers, and laptops to do e-shopping and banking, yet they end up exhausted by the end of the day. What's wrong with this picture? We're trying to do too much and do it in less time. The question is, are we really are getting more done? So, let's talk about it.

Slowing down allows you to be more focused on what you're doing. It helps you to stay in the present and enjoy where you are right now. It also gives the mind time to receive information that allows you to be more efficient. It takes conscience effort to slow down, and it needs to become a habit. You have to think about the pace you're currently functioning in and then decide if you're moving too fast or not. One way to determine if you're moving too fast is if you're experiencing that anxiety you feel when you're rushing. Rushing causes me to feel stressed when there is nothing to be stressed about. It's uncomfortable. When you feel yourself rushing, simply stop, take a deep breath, then begin again at an exaggeratedly slow pace. It's going to feel weird initially but trust that you will start to feel better and less hurried. Sometimes my pace is so slow that I'm almost still. I'm moving, but my movements are more deliberate and focused. This is a constant battle in a hurried world, but trust me you'll feel much better and be more relaxed if you take your time.

As a teacher rounding with residents at 7:15 AM then getting to clinic by 8:30 to see patients there's always the temptation to rush. I hate being late, and I really hate it when patients have to wait though often it's inevitable. I finish rounds late, then start clinic late, and now I'm tempted to rush through each patient to get to the next patient. I feel stressed and the patient doesn't get the time they deserve with me. The best thing I've found to do is accept that I am behind schedule and slow down to give each patient my full attention and time. I can enjoy helping a patient unrushed, and they get their needs meant without being rushed.

There are certain times when I have to hurry, such as when a mother or her unborn child is in immediate danger. I can go into overdrive and get a baby out by cesarean section in less than a minute. But I try to reserve my speed for emergencies only.

Another one of my biggest battles has been to eat slowly. Eating fast is a habit I developed during my residency. I never knew when my beeper was going to go off and I'd have to get up and leave my food, so I got into the habit of eating rapidly so that I finished before being paged. I still catch myself doing this when I go to a restaurant. You want to savor your meal. Take time to enjoy the experience. We often have the time to slow down and enjoy life, but we simply get caught up in the rush. We eat fast out of habit. This habit can be exchanged for the new habit of eating slowly.

One of the reasons I found for procrastinating is my desire to get the job done too fast. I usually want to get the task done now or I want the task done but don't want to put the time in to complete the task. Because I didn't like that rushed feeling, I would procrastinate to avoid it. I would procrastinate, not because the project was so daunting but because I had placed the stress of getting it done quickly on myself rather than deciding to take my time and enjoy the process. You have to be careful that your desire for speed doesn't prevent you from taking action to achieve worthwhile goals. Don't be so caught up in the goal that you don't enjoy the process that leads to your goal. People often talk about enjoying the journey, or stopping to smell the roses or the coffee. This is great advice for achieving any goal. So, slow down and smell the roses. Take your time and enjoy studying if you're in school. We are in so much of a hurry to get things done that we constantly miss out on life *right now*. You have to figure out ways to slow down and savor this super gift called life, and that means taking the time to enjoy the most mundane of tasks. Remember, all of us are one heartbeat away from death. Savor this moment.

I grew up having to do the dishes with my sister after dinner every night. I usually washed and she dried the dishes. Now that I'm married it is no big deal for me to clean up the kitchen after meals, and I figured out a way to enjoy the process. I simply take my time and get totally into the moment. I make a conscious effort to *take my time* and savor the moment. I think you'll find that most of your stress is related to unrealistic expectations you've placed on yourself regarding how fast something can or should be done. If you would allow yourself to slow down you would enjoy what you're doing much more and with less stress.

When I make rounds I take my time. This allows me to be more efficient and still get done in a reasonable period of time. Sometimes we're working so fast that we may not be working as efficiently as we should because we haven't taken the time to evaluate what we're doing and why. Sometimes we need to stop and see if we need to be working as fast as we are. This should definitely be done if the pace is stressing us out. We start to think about what we're going to do next rather than focusing on the task at hand. Sometimes we end up having to redo tasks that were done incorrectly because of our haste.

Haven't you been in such a hurry to go somewhere only to forget your keys or some important papers you needed that day, but your mind was rushing so much that you didn't remember until you were out of the house and on your way. If you had not been rushing you would have heard your conscience reminding you to get those keys or papers before you left the house. We're moving too fast, folks.

Slow Down

This rapid pace causes us to be stressed, forgetful, and anxious. We find ourselves being irritable and uptight not so much because of the job, but the pace at which we perform the job. Whenever you decide to get a certain amount of work done in a given period of time you need to assess whether you've given yourself a reasonable amount of time to get the job done.

When I decided to write a book I didn't have any idea how long it could take until I started reading about writers and realized it could take a year or more to get a book written. If I hadn't acquired that knowledge I could have become disillusioned or discouraged because I hadn't finished my book in three to six months. Placing unrealistic time tables on achieving your goals is a setup for failure. We also tend to place too much on our plates to do, and if anyone suggests we add anything else to it we feel like exploding. This gets into learning how to say no to certain tasks and putting first things first. Some of us try to do more in a day than can be done comfortably and enjoyed. You are in control of how fast you walk, talk, write, eat, drink, mow the lawn, clean the dishes, and on and on. If you need to read the paper for the latest stock quotes then give yourself ample time to do that. You may have to get up earlier to be able to take advantage of the morning quiet. The beauty of getting up at 4:00 or 5:00 AM and working is that others may still be asleep and this is your opportunity to do what you need to do at your pace, and I suggest it be a slow pace. I know this may go against the type A personality a lot of us have, but you'll find that you'll enjoy life much more on slow mode versus fast mode.

We can't slow time down, but we *can* slow ourselves down. We do have enough time but we have to prioritize our time and do what's most important within the time allotted to us. You have to decide how important watching television is in helping you to reach your goals. I like watching television in small doses. I'll watch college football on Saturday and *Sixty Minutes* occasionally on Sunday night and maybe two more hours of a favorite show my wife likes to watch and that's it. After football season I'll probably watch even less. I'm tempted to not watch any television if I think it's interfering with the time I need to get something done. I use television to allow my mind to float off into nowhere land. I would rather read a self-development book.

You have to constantly take stock of what may be interfering with your time. Is television worth your time right now or is it using time you could use to work on your goals. If you gave up one hour-long TV show a day for 365 days and used that same time to read, write, or work on your self-development, you would grow tremendously. You could get a book written with an extra 365 hours added to your life simply by giving up one hour of television.

Success takes time, and we have only twenty-four hours to use each day. If we subtract eight hours for sleep that leaves sixteen hours of wake time. If you use three of those for television now you're left with thirteen hours. Let's say we use thirty minutes getting ready for work and another thirty minutes getting ready for bed. Now we have twelve hours left. You have to eat so take off two hours for eating and being social. Some of us eat on the run so we may not need that much time. You now have ten hours and many people have to spend seven or eight of them at their jobs. Wow, you now have two hours of "do what you want to do time." Wait a minute; you need thirty minutes to exercise, so now you have one and a half hours. You have one and a half hours to read, write, or work on your particular project. Of course, if you eliminate two of those television hours you now have three and a half hours to get a lot of work done. I know, what about homework with the kids, little league practice, soccer practice, and taking the kids all over the place after school. We may need to take that other hour of television away if you're still raising children. Let's slow down and take stock of our time.

1. Sleep   8 hours
2. Television   1 hour
3. Prepare for work and bed   1 hour
4. Eating/social time   2 hours
5. Job   8 hours
6. Exercise/meditation/prayer   1 hour
                                   Twenty-one hours

You still have three hours to spare, and if you knock out the other hour of television you have four hours to use toward your goals. If you have children you'll probably need to use at least two of those hours for homework. If they're preschool this time could be used to

Slow Down

read to the little ones. You may not use two hours for socializing or eating but you can see how there is time to get things done if you prioritize your time.

The above time schedule is simply an example of where time might be used during a five-day workweek. We have even more time on the weekend if we don't overbook ourselves. The bottom line is that you have time out there to work on your goals, but you need to take stock of where your time is going and then prioritize it. You can slow down if you limit your time to what's important and give up some of your television time if you currently watch a lot of TV.

I've found that the best time to practice being slow is when no other demands are placed on me. An athlete practices his sport regularly in order to be good at it. If you want to be good at taking your time and slowing down to be successful, you will need to practice. The best time to practice is when you are alone with no other distractions. Just like a professional team that goes behind closed doors to work out, that's what you need to do if you want this new habit to become natural for you. You'll also have to have the courage to develop this habit, trusting that it will aid you toward your success. You'll need discipline to make yourself purposely be slower and develop this habit. It won't be easy because we live in a fast paced world and we'll often be tempted to jump in the rush because it feels exciting to rush around feeling like we are getting things done when really we're not. You have to trust the process. Taking your time and knowing your business or job well or taking the time to improve your skills at whatever you do brings fulfillment and ultimately success if coupled with a good game plan. Of course you need to take your time to formulate a plan, so stop the rush.

You will catch yourself in hurry mode and when you do, don't beat yourself up about it. Just stop, take a deep breath and get back on track. Remember, a professional athlete, musician, or actor is constantly practicing to get better. They have to practice to simply maintain their current level of competence. Professional musicians may practice up to eight hours a day. If they want to be the best, they know they have to put the time in. If you want to be the best, and reach your potential, you will have to put the time in. In order for me to act slowly and methodically, I have to practice being slow. I have to constantly work at writing, reading, talking, operating, and walking slowly. It's a battle, but it's worth it because you'll feel more relaxed and in control of your time and life. Remember, the tortoise beat the hare.

It takes time to comprehend and understand what you read. I used to try and speed read but for me I didn't comprehend or enjoy what I was reading. If you've taken a speed-reading course and it works for you, then by all means keep doing what you are doing, but if you are a slow reader don't sweat it. Focus on understanding and applying what you read. Enjoy the process. You can't speed-read physics, calculus, or organic chemistry—classes that will eat you alive if you try to rush through them. It's not possible. Take your time. Some people elect not to read because they keep telling themselves they read too slow or that they're a slow reader. Hey, news flash, nobody knows how fast or slow you read, and who cares as long as you learn what you need to learn.

When I was in college I knew it took me a little longer to finish the test compared to some of my classmates, but it didn't matter because I still managed to finish the test and pass the test. No one is going to ask you how long it took you to get your degree or achieve most of your goals. The bottom line is you reached the goal. As long as my residents pass the test, I could care less how long it took them to read the material. Take your time and get it done.

Part of slowing down to be successful is to realize that it takes time to be good at anything. You have to allow yourself to be bad at first and then work your way up to being better. It takes years to be great at something and the ones who become great weren't able to take any shortcuts. Most doctors will take four years to finish medical school. Most lawyers will take three years to finish law school. Of course, that doesn't include the usual four years of college prior to that. Artist, musicians, and athletes take years to become proficient at what they do. I wish I could play the piano well enough to put on a concert tour, but it would take years of practice for that to occur and I am not willing at this time of my life to do that. I don't have the time to dedicate myself to that much practice, but if I did I would realize that it was going to take years for me to be a good piano player.

You can place a lot of unnecessary stress on yourself if you place unrealistic expectations on yourself. Being frustrated because you can't hit a down the line forehand like Andre Agassi or a chip shot like Tiger Woods when they have hit thousands of those shots in practice is being unrealistic. You too will have to hit your share of forehands and chip shots if you ever want to be as good as them. You have to slow down and take stock of what it takes to be good and then be willing to pay the dues necessary to be good. I play golf very infrequently and when I first started playing I took a few lessons then went out to the driving range to practice. I would get better, but if I didn't get out on a regular basis I would start hitting poorly again. I wouldn't get too upset about it because this was supposed to be my relaxation time. Then I noted that the best golfers in the world have a personal coach usually watching every swing. The best golfers practice before each round and may practice again after their round. I decided to be content with just being outdoors on the course away from my job. It would be crazy for me to get upset about missing a shot that I had not even practiced. If I wanted to be good at golf I was going to have to put in a tremendous amount of time into practicing. Most people are not willing to put in the time to be great at something. If you are willing to be that person, then the sky is the limit for you. Just know that it takes time, and it can be a slow process. You are capable of doing great things; the question is whether you are willing to pay the dues. The dues are usually time and effort. Take your time, put in the time, slow down, and be the success I know you can be.

Chapter Ten

It's On You

It's on you. You are accountable for your success. Just like you are accountable for certain past failures and successes, it's all up to you. If you have failed at something in the past, and we all have, you need to examine how you caused the failure and not look for ways to place blame on others or on your environment. Once you take ownership for your failures it's easier to take ownership for your successes. You must decide to take control of your destiny, knowing that you can't wait for luck or breaks to be successful. You'll have to make your own breaks, and create your own luck.

When I made a decision to go to medical school I knew that it was up to me to fill out the applications, apply for student loans, and go on the interviews. My parents gave encouragement, but it was on me to take the necessary action to get into medical school. You may be considering going back to school, and the only thing stopping you is you. You won't take the entrance exam, or look into grants or scholarships because you are for waiting for what? What are you waiting for? Have you ever stopped to ask yourself what you're waiting for? You have to be accountable for your life.

When you accept accountability for your success you are taking control of your destiny, and you stop waiting for luck or some other person or thing to make success happen for you. You are now the one in control. This gives you power. You can't play the victim and you won't be a victim. You'll be a victor instead.

Some people blame other races, religions, cultures, genders, or any number of people or circumstances for their current life situation. Playing the blame game doesn't take you out of your situation. You have to take yourself out of your current situation. As long as you're constantly looking for excuses you'll be using up precious time that could be better spent planning how you can move out of your current situation. It's not easy, and success isn't about easy, it's about hard work.

Success Is About Hard Work

Taking responsibility requires self examination, and in examining yourself you can grow from whatever mistakes you may have made. To state that you made a mistake, then examine why the mistake was made allows for growth to occur. Owning up to our mistakes provides an opportunity for growth. Growth takes place each time you accept your responsibility for your actions and learn from those actions, whether they were appropriate or not.

In my first marriage I was not very good at balancing my home life with family life. I placed medicine over my marriage rather than putting medicine on hold long enough to get my marriage back on tract. After my divorce, the first thing I decided to do was take a good look at myself and how I could have been a better husband. For me to spend a lot of time blaming my ex-wife, medicine, God, or any other entity would have been a waste of time. I had to look myself in the mirror and decide to be better in my next marriage. I didn't want to repeat the same mistakes. I had to take responsibility for the failed marriage and learn as much as possible from the experience. If I hadn't taken responsibility for my failed marriage, I would be at risk for repeating the same thing in my current marriage. This is why it's so important to be accountable for your mistakes and learn from them so that you don't repeat them over and over again.

If you are an adult, you can't afford to not be responsible. Our children, grandchildren, and colleagues need to know that we will take ownership for what happens in our homes and on our jobs. A husband needs to assure his wife that he will take the blame for events in the house that he's responsible for. A chief executive officer is accountable for the actions of her company leadership and the success or failure of her company. When you are accountable you have the opportunity to grow from your successes and failures. This can be stressful and scary. However, this is a more rewarding way to live.

Success-What Does It Take?

Every time I pick up a scalpel, I know that I am about to make a permanent scar on my patient. I need to make it straight, and I want it to heal with the least amount of scarring as possible. I'm anxious because I am the one accountable for the incision I'm about to make. Surgeons have to get past being anxious about operating or at least learn how to perform in spite of this anxiety. We have to be decisive, and be totally responsible for what we do with our hands in the operating room. We have to become acquainted with that thought of what if I make a mistake, or harm the patient. We have to own up to it.

When you decide to be accountable for your actions, you make better decisions and you're more likely to learn more from your mistakes because you know that you will be accountable for your next decision.

Katie Spotz is the first woman to cross the Atlantic Ocean by herself. She traveled over 2,800 miles in a row boat from Senegal, West Africa, to Georgetown, Guyana, by herself. Nobody else was accountable for her success but her. Just think about how small a cruise ship becomes when it's out in the middle of the ocean. Now think of yourself in a row boat five hundred miles from shore, and it's up to your two arms to get you back to shore. The rowing was all on Katie. She challenged herself to do what was necessary to cross that sea. Most of us are not going to make a decision to cross an ocean, but we may decide to start a business, and the work needed to get that business off the ground will take the fortitude you would have to have to cross an ocean. There's a strong desire within most of us to do something outstanding, but the work and energy it takes to accomplish great things is more than what most are willing to expend.

Amelia Earhart was the first woman to fly across the Atlantic Ocean, and she made an attempt to circumnavigate the world. Again, here is an individual who chose a goal and against many odds went after that goal. People like Spotz and Earhart take life on with all of its risk of failure and disappointment. They decide that it's on them to accomplish the task, and they are accountable for their success or failure. Going after your goals knowing that you could fail and risking failure is what makes life exciting.

I practiced medicine in Atlanta, Georgia, for nineteen years before I made the decision to leave the city and look for other opportunities. My wife and I had a lot of anxiety about leaving a city where we had our church home, friends, and family. We had to see it as an adventure that would pay off with continued career fulfillment and financial stability. If things didn't work out I would see it as a learning experience and look for an even better opportunity. When you take charge of your future and decide to be accountable for your actions, you tend to make decisions that yield the results you want and you take advantage of your successes and failures. If you own your failures you have the opportunity to use them to your advantage. When you see the future as an adventure waiting to happen rather than a time of fear and anxiety you will start to live a much richer life.

I never looked at the consequences of missing a big shot... when you think about the consequences you always think of a negative result.
—Michael Jordan

When you decide to be accountable for your success or failure, you are no longer as fearful or concerned about outcomes because you know that you can handle either one. If you are successful, that's great; if you fail that's no big deal because you're going to use that failure to make better decisions the next time. Successful people don't allow themselves to be victims because they remain in control of their response to both success and failure. This is especially important when it comes to responding to failure. Achievers account for their failures by taking a close look at what went wrong and then making the appropriate adjustments. They don't have time for whining. Achievers are busy planning and acting out their next move. This is a habit of thinking that you have to develop and that can be developed with practice. This is also a decision point for you. You have to decide that your life is to be run by you and not by every circumstance that comes your way.

It's important for you to constantly work on being better. We all are a work in progress, and it takes conscious effort to work on being better. You will need to read about successful people and how they overcame adversity and dealt with problems. You will need to develop a habit of seeing problems as opportunities for you to grow. Each time you conquer a problem, you grow. You want to see yourself as a problem solver and develop an attitude that says-"bring it on."

At this writing, the country is supposed to be in a recession. That may be true, but you can't allow your mental attitude to be in a recession or a depression. Remember, you are accountable for your personal economy (budget), mind set, and well being. For those of you who are believers in God, you are responsible for your spiritual growth. You are accountable for that man or woman you see in the mirror who keeps bugging you to write a book, finish school, ask for that raise, or take charge of that project. Bottom line, it's on you. The fairy godmother is not showing up. Wishing is not going to take you to the next level. You taking charge and doing what needs to be done is what will lead you to success.

I think a lot of people have unrealistic expectations regarding what it takes to be successful. They watch television and see beautiful people with beautiful homes, cars, and clothes, yet they don't see anybody working to make the money that it takes to buy the big house or stylish car. I think there are some people who think that stuff simply appears. The bottom line is that most millionaires work hard for the money and deal with a certain amount of stress to get it. There are doctors and lawyers who have six figure salaries, but they don't make that kind of money only working 40 hours a week. The backdrop of anyone who makes a lot of money is usually hard work and sacrifice. Let's dismiss the myth right now. Rich people have to work hard and put in a lot of hours as well as deal with multiple stresses to make money. As a rich person I know that I have to make a decision to have nice things, make a certain income, and be willing to pay the price to get them. Many people don't have because they don't decide to have, and they're not willing to pay the price to have. The price is different for everyone and its all relative.

You could be in a dead end job, and it would require you to go to night school or take online cases to position yourself for a better career but that would require loss of sleep, fear of failure, and besides none of your coworkers are making any sacrifices so why should you. You are in charge of your destiny, and you know I'm going to say it.

You're Not Going To Feel Like It.
So just do it.
DO IT WITH YOUR LIP POKED OUT.

Life is not about feeling good all the time; however you'll be surprised at how much better you'll feel once you start taking charge of your life and doing what needs to be done. There is less stress associated with action in the direction of your goals than sitting around wishing something would happen in your life.

Eventually you won't have to do it with your lip poked out because you will see the results of your labor. You might even smile a little. Bottom line, you will have to expend a lot of energy moving yourself from a boring dead-end job to the career that you want to have. You will take yourself to a whole different level of person. Every time you take charge of your life and say yes to those actions that are demanding but worthwhile, you end up growing. If you're not feeling a little stress or anxiety periodically you're probably stuck in a comfort zone that's keeping you from growing. Even a plant has to push through a covering of dirt. For some reason accomplishing great things come with some pain and discomfort. Think of childbirth. You are one of the greatest wonders of all, and you came through the pains of childbirth experienced by your mother. Yes, you are a miracle. You are worthwhile and capable of greatness but you can't be a wimp. This life will not give you what you want without you making a decision to go after what you want. You can achieve and have many things, but you have to pay the price. I couldn't become a physician in two years; it takes four years. Law school takes three years. It might take you six years to get your masters'; so what, once you have it, you have it. Nobody is going to ask you how long it took you to get it. I don't ask students how many times they applied to medical school before they got accepted or whether they got in the first time or not. I just want to know if they finished school. Are they ready to work hard and take good care of people?

Knowing that it's on you should be liberating, but you have to accept the initial discomfort that almost always comes with making a decision to be better and get what you want. Once you take on responsibility, you will start to think differently. You will begin to create in your mind different ways to achieve your goals versus wasting time waiting for lady luck or wishing for things to change. It ain't gonna change unless you make it change. Life is a great gift, but life will not spoil you. It demands that you expend the necessary energy to get up and get going.

Every morning I get up to exercise I have to deal with the same resistance I felt when I first started. The difference is that I recognize the resistance for what it is. My mind doesn't want to get up and exercise, and it doesn't want my body to expend the energy of walking to the bathroom to get dressed and get out the door to drive to the gym. I have learned to ignore the mind and my body's resistance and simply get into motion. It's on me. When the alarm goes off, I immediately get up. I can't give my mind time to talk me out of getting up.

You are not your mind. Your mind is a great tool that you have to train and bring under your control. Your mind will tell you all kinds of false information and create fears that in no way could ever happen, yet we listen to this mind and allow it to keep us from taking action toward our goals. Try getting up tomorrow to go for a brisk walk or get on a stationary bike. Tomorrow morning your mind will create all kinds of reasons why you should lie back down and go to sleep. You'll have aches and pains you didn't have the night before all because you have decided to get up and go exercise. This happens with other tasks as well. I like the technique subscribed to by Mel Robbins, author of the book *Stop Saying You're Fine*. She talks about using the five-second rule. As soon as you get an idea to do something, don't ruminate over it; start doing it within five seconds. Don't give your mind enough time to create a barrage of negativity, and don't give your body enough time to wallow in its minor aches and pains. Get up and get moving. Remember, it's on you. Don't sit and ponder about how you feel. Be the strong human being you are.

You're not a wimp; you just seem to act like one more than you should. Take back the responsibility for your life. Do what you know you need to do and tell your mind to get over it. I would say to tell your mind and body to "get a life" but they already have one and it's yours. You want to get in the habit of telling your life partners(mind and body) what you want to do, where you are going to go, and how long you plan to be there when you get there. Once you get into this habit you will start to enjoy life much more. You won't feel as

It's On You

if you're being tossed about by the wind and subject to the feelings of the hour. You will be able to make a statement that you are going to do something, and your body will know you mean it—therefore there's no need in creating negativity or any aches and pains. If the negative feelings come and the false aches develop it won't matter because the powerful you acts in spite of the mind/body drama. You are now the architect of your life.

Conclusion

If there is any one lesson that I want you to grasp and hold tightly to, it is that everything I've talked about requires persistent work on a daily basis. Being successful is a full time job. You never reach a point where you get to rest on past achievements until you are out of the game. Michael Jordan can rest on his NBA titles, but if he were to try and play professional basketball again just one year after retiring, he would have to go back to training as hard if not harder to get back to his pre-retirement state. To stay at the top and remain at the top requires considerable vigilance. Tennis great Pete Sampras was the number one player in the world for 286 weeks. That's over five years. It takes considerable work to maintain that level of play. If you look at Tiger Woods, you'll see a consistency that comes only from hard work, perseverance, and success habits.

If you are in the corporate world, medicine, education, law, or any other profession, it requires persistent hard work to stay at the top of your game. It takes courage and discipline every day. I think discipline is the most important ingredient because it's required to develop all the other characteristics needed for continued success. You will have to make yourself be mindful of where you are and where you want to be. You need to plan for your own success. Success will not simply fall in your lap. There is no overnight success, but there can be success if you take a night to plan out where you want to be this time next month, next year, or five years from now. Taking a night to determine what you are willing to sacrifice to be the best at what you do. Getting up a little earlier, watching less television, and doing what you know you should do will take you to the next level.

I think a lot of people want to reach certain goals in life but they don't realize how much work it takes and how hard it will

Success-What Does It Take?

be. If a person thinks something will be easy and it turns out to be hard, they get discouraged. I wrote the chapter about life being hard because it is, and sometimes knowing that up front prepares you to tackle life better. If a sports team knows that their next game is against the number one team in the league, they make a decision to practice much harder that week in preparation for a tough opponent. We have a tough opponent everyday whether we like it or not, and that opponent is life itself. Sometimes I view life as a prizefighter standing over me like Mohammad Ali with boxing gloves on, ready to knock me back into bed as I try to get up. You and I have to get up swinging every day. You have to fight your way to the gym, or away from that piece of dessert. You have to battle your old habits as you struggle to develop new ones.

You will be in constant battle with yourself and life. I struggle to get out of bed every morning at 5:00 AM. It doesn't matter that I got eight hours of sleep or not. If I'm waking up to go to the gym or to work, it's often a struggle. Now, if I'm waking up to catch a flight to the beach, I jump up and I'm ready to go, but it's always a little struggle to get going in the morning for me. I do my best writing and reading in the morning, but I have to battle the procrastination demon like anyone else. I have to constantly remind myself of what my goals are and what I need to do to achieve them. That's why you hear so much about planning and goal setting, because goals act as a catalyst to action and that catalyst coupled with discipline leads to success. Life rewards disciplined consistent action.

It's important that you read something every day that reminds you to stay in the game. You should constantly be reading books that lead to self-development. Read books on leadership, fear, courage, goal setting, discipline, habits, and any books in your field of work that help you to work better. Write down quotes that inspire you from people of high achievement and read them regularly. You want to saturate yourself with positive messages and surround yourself with positive people. I keep three-by-five cards with reminders of how I want to be, and how hard work is needed to achieve my goals. I have to be constantly reminded that I can't let my current feelings interfere with my work. I keep a card in my pocket and on my desk with similar information, reminding me of who I need to be. I'm not

Conclusion

perfect and being perfect is not the goal, but being consistent about following a plan is the goal.

All of us are constantly being bombarded with negativity from multiple sources, so to counter balance this negativity we have to feed ourselves positive messages every day. I can't over emphasize that you have to do this *every day*. It needs to be your new way of life. This is a success habit you must develop. You have to feed your mind and spirit with positive reminders every day. You can't leave a manicured lawn alone one week without weeds trying to come in and destroy the lawn. It's the same with success habits. You have to keep the negativity out. I keep a three-by-five card in my pocket that has eleven lines containing reminders geared to keep me on track. Here they are:

1. Don't be perfect; perfectionism kills action.
2. Slow down.
3. Take action to change feelings.
4. Be present.
5. Courage, discipline, integrity, commitment.
6. Do what you don't feel like doing.
7. Break through the wall.
8. Time boxing.
9. Let discipline determine your feelings.
10. Work when at work.
11. Plan your life.

You may create a different list that works best for you, but the key is that you create and carry this list with you all the time and read it every day. I try to read mine three times a day because I feed my body at least that much therefore I feed my mind the way I feed my body. This is in addition to continually reading to develop myself—and reading to stay current in my profession. I also read a spiritual devotional every day. Don't leave spiritual growth out of the equation. There's more to you than flesh and blood.

All of the above requires you to make a decision. You have to decide what kind of life you want for yourself; then be prepared to constantly pay the price to have that life. It's all on you as stated before, and I have confidence that you can design a great life for

Success-What Does It Take?

yourself, but you have to want it for yourself. Please do what you hear and see successful people do in order to be successful. Remember, if you do what successful people do over and over again, you can have the same results. Get started now. God bless you.

About the Author

Dr. Kendall M. Handy is an instructor and teacher of obstetrics and gynecology at The Medical Center in Columbus, Georgia. He has been training medical students, physician assistants, and both family practice and obstetrical residents for over twenty years. One of his primary objectives is not just to teach medicine, but to teach future medical students and others the importance of self-development. His formal educational background includes High Point College (now University), Alabama A and M University, The University of Alabama School of Medicine, and a residency in Obstetrics and Gynecology at Sinai Hospital in Baltimore, Maryland.